Living on a
Rolling Stone

PATTY HODGE MARI

authorHOUSE®

AuthorHouse™
1663 Liberty Drive
Bloomington, IN 47403
www.authorhouse.com
Phone: 1 (800) 839-8640

Published by AuthorHouse   01/06/2016

ISBN: 978-1-5049-5456-3 (sc)
ISBN: 978-1-5049-5455-6 (e)

Library of Congress Control Number: 2015916507

Print information available on the last page.

Introduction

This is the life story of a man and a woman who saw, felt, and breathed the tragedy of loss in their lives and yet managed to find love, happiness, and purpose in spite of it all. Through it all, they struggled to understand who they were and the reason for their existence.

In researching John's ancestors, there seemed to be a great deal of secrecy about who his mother was. The family was told she was an unwanted child whose mother had left her on the doorstep of the Catholic Church in Italy, with no birth or baptism certificates or any identification of who the baby belonged to or who had left the child there. It has always been a mystery—was this true, or was she really was born to the mother who raised her and brought her to the United States from Italy? How old was she? Family members say they thought she was about three. No one had ever seen this child before. From the stories told by the extended family, she was not treated as nicely as the other children in the family.

Would John ever find the answers to such a puzzled background? Would there ever be a time of real peace and understanding concerning his mother?

As a Christian, John wondered what purpose God had to allow this to be. Is He, the God of the universe, concerned only with our eternal destiny, or is He a personal God who looks after and provides protection and love to His children? Would God grant his request for an answer to the mystery his heart had so longed for?

Part I

Learenazo Constantine Mari and wife Rosa (Tozzi)

Chapter 1

Papa

Learenazo Constantine Mari and his wife, Rosa (Tozzi) Mari, lived in the village of Ischia di Castro, Italy. On June 7, 1887, a newborn's cries were heard through the bedroom door of the Mari home. Rosa's prayers had been answered—she had given birth to a healthy boy. Learenazo was happy too. He had a son he would name Gulio. *Mari* was a good name, Learenazo often told Gulio as a boy. Rosa explained, "It means by the sea," as she told him stories and sang songs about the sea. As the boy grew, his parents knew their son would grow up to be very adventurous.

All through his childhood, Gulio Mari listened as the men in the tiny village told stories about the great country of America. "It is a country of great freedom and opportunity," one would say.

"Where every man has a job. Yes, a good job and good pay," another villager would add.

Another would chime in, saying, "It is nothing to have hundreds of dollars and to own land and a house for your family."

The stories went on and on. One by one, the men of the village left their wives and children and sailed to America with the promise of obtaining work and a home. Then they would send for their families.

Gulio dreamed of the day he would be old enough to board a ship headed for America. Learenazo died when Gulio was yet a child, and as the only son, he was expected to take on financial responsibility for the family. Gulio was nineteen when his mother gave her adventurous son her blessings to go to America. He promised he would send her money, and as soon as he was financially able, he would send for her so she too could live in the land of plenty.

Gulio was soon aboard the SS *Princess Irene* and on his way to the New World—the United States of America. As the shores of New York City came into sight, the passengers erupted in cheers of joy and thanksgiving for their safe journey. As they docked at Ellis Island, they gasped in amazement at the Statue of Liberty. Men took off their hats and placed them over their hearts. Women aboard cried with pride and joy at the beauty and promise of America. It was November 18, 1906. With both fear and hope for the future, Gulio Mari stepped from the ship onto American soil.

Gulio went to a section of New York City where other Italian immigrants had settled, his native tongue was spoken, and the food was familiar. However, it didn't take long for him to realize that the dream of the good life would not be as easy to achieve as he had thought. He wasn't permitted to linger in New York City without a job.

At the time, coal-mining companies and the steel industry were seeking immigrants to work for them. Instead of mining gold in California, as he heard some men did, Gulio found himself in a small coal-mining community in West Virginia. The coal company owned many mines in several states, and men were often were transferred from one mine to another, even from one state to another, wherever they were needed. The work was hard and dirty. There was no safety equipment and no union to protect the men. They worked from before dawn until dark and were given little pay.

Because of the frequent transfers, men couldn't call any place home. Miners generally lived in a boardinghouse, as Gulio did for several years. The coal company built and owned the houses where the miners and their families lived. Most food and merchandise were purchased from the company store, which the coal company also owned. These practices meant most of the money miners earned ended up back in the hands of the coal company.

Gulio tried to rent a house in West Virginia. He was told he could rent a room but not a house. This was to keep Italians from settling there permanently. He felt this was not fair. He had been told in Italy that the United States was a good and fair country where he had the right to the good life. He wanted so badly to send for his mother but finally decided not to dwell on the present but plan for the future. He didn't want to return to Italy. So Gulio knew he must search until he found a place he could call home.

After several years, Gulio had saved enough money to send for his mother. She was old now and afraid of the long voyage alone, but she so longed to see her son again. Her daughters were married and had their own families. They encouraged their mother to go.

Just as she was about to board the ship, Rosa had a stroke and died. Gulio wept when the news reached him. Never again would he see his mother. He had not kept his promise to bring her to America, and he was so sad. He mourned his mother's death for many years. He showed no interest in women or marriage; he simply worked. For pleasure he played cards, smoked cigars, and made and drank good Italian wine.

By now he had worked many years for the same coal company and was able to stay in Pennsylvania. He lived in the little town of Ernest and worked the Ernest mines as well as other mines in the area. Ernest was a town with nearly every European country represented. Immigrants from Italy, Poland, Germany, France, Yugoslavia, and others made it their home.

And the angel of his presence saved them. Isa. 63 : 9.

The angel of the Lord encampeth round about them that fear him, and delivereth them. Ps. 33 : 7.

Be not forgetful to entertain strangers: for thereby some have entertained angels. Heb. 13 : 2.

Thy Word is a lamp unto my feet and a light unto my path. Ps. 119 : 105.

Are they not all ministering spirits sent forth to minister for them who shall be heirs of salvation? Heb. 1 : 14.

❧ A MINER'S PRAYER ❧

O Lord after I have worked my last day and come out of the earth and have placed my feet on Thy footstool, let me use the tools of prudence, faith, hope and charity. From now on till I will be called to sign my last pay roll, make all the cables in the machinery strong with Thy love. Supply all the gangways, slopes and chambers with the pure air of Thy grace and let the light of hope be my guidance, and when my last picking and shoveling is done, may my last car be full of Thy grace and give me the Holy Bible for my last shift, so that Thou, the General Superintendent of all the collieries, can say: "Well done, thou good, faithful miner, come and sign the pay roll and receive the check of eternal happiness." Amen.

And God shall wipe away all tears from their eyes ; and there shall be no more death, neither sorrow, nor crying, neither shall there be any more pain: for the former things are passed away. Rev. 21 : 4.

Old things are passed away; behold all things are become new. II Cor. 5 : 17.

Price 10 cents. Sent postpaid on receipt of price.
Address

C. ERB, YORK, PA.

AGENTS WANTED!

Mama

On March 5, 1905, somewhere in Salerno, Italy, a baby girl was born. No one seemed to know who this child's parents were and why she was left on the steps of the Catholic church. Is this story even true? Maybe so; maybe not. Some say Raphaela (Linardo) Cuozzo, who cared for this baby, was really her mother. The child's name was Giovannina. *Giovannina what?* many wondered. Was she adopted? Did she have a birth or baptism certificate? No one knows.

The story goes that Raphaela migrated to the United States in 1908, bringing little Giovannina with her. Raphaela came to join her husband, Donald Cuozzo, who had immigrated in 1904. After she came to the United States, Giovannina's name was changed to Jenny.

The family settled in the town of Fulton Run, a small coal-mining town in Pennsylvania. Donald was a coal miner and worked the many mines in that area. He and Raphaela had three children: Rosie, Thomas, and Donald Jr. (nicknamed Doly). Donald Cuozzo Sr. died in 1911 at the age of forty.

A year later, Raphaela married Tony Bevaqua. They had a daughter they named Mary. Tony was said to be a very stern man, and he insisted all the children carry his name. So Jenny, Rosie, Doly, and Thomas's last name was changed to Bevaqua—not legally, but by Mr. Bevaqua. How do we know it wasn't legal? When Donald went into the army, he was sent back to Pennsylvania to find out what his correct name was. To his surprise, it was Donald Cuozzo.

A story is told that one day when Jenny was playing with the other children, a rock was thrown into a tree to knock down apples. The rock hit Jenny on top of her head. As a result, Jenny had terrible headaches from time to time. Apparently, she was never given any medical care. Even if she had been, there were no tests available to indicate that Jenny had a serious problem. No one knew until much later that a blood clot had developed on her brain.

This is Julius and Jenny Mari.
There is no date to tell when this was taken.

This house, #90 in Ernest, Pennsylvania, was rented to Julius Mari for his family and to furnish room and board to other miners from about 1921 to sometime in the 1940s. The house has a new owner, and it has been beautifully refinished. What a joy to see the love and care the owners have given it.

Chapter 2

Gulio was thirty-three and Jenny was sixteen when they met. They married on January 21, 1921, and rented a company house in Ernest, not far from Jenny's family in Fulton Run. To help pay the rent, Gulio and Jenny took in boarders. This was a great responsibility for a sixteen-year-old girl. She cooked and baked for her family as well as all the boarders. Plus, she cleaned all the rooms and washed and ironed all the clothes, including what the men wore in the coal mines. It was almost more than she could handle. Jenny's younger sister, Rosie, who lived with her parents, helped out, especially when Jenny was pregnant.

Family

Gulio and Jenny's first child, Josephine, was born on December 7, 1922. Costantino was born October 26, 1924, and then Edward on September 30, 1926. Rose Marie was born May 24, 1928; Julia on December 14, 1929; John on January 31, 1932; Constance, called Connie, on October 30, 1933; Thomas on March 24, 1936; and Fredrick on October 13, 1939. As the number of children increased, there was less room for boarders and less energy for Jenny.

Julius Mari holding John, Josephine (the oldest child), and Edward
First row: Rose Marie, Julia, Louie Rigato, and Connie

Jenny Mari holding her son John, age three, and Connie, age two.

Jenny worked hard to provide her family's many needs, and she wasn't a well woman. Each time she was in labor with another child, the tiny blood clot pressed on her brain, causing terrible headaches, depression, and confusion.

The Mari family and other residents of the little community experienced good times and bad times. The women baked pies and sold them at church bazaars—except for the ones placed on the church windowsills to cool and stolen by mischievous boys. Children played in the woods around the community. There were huge grapevines to swing from and trees and rocks to hide behind. There were wonderful ballgames down at the diamond. Everyone remembered Alonzo Hicks, a young black man who could hit the ball farther than anyone could imagine.

With so many children, there weren't any luxuries. Gulio never had a car, and none of the children had toys or games to play with. There was no Christmas tree or gifts to open. Santa Claus only visited rich families, and the Maris didn't know any.

Meals were very simple. Gulio made polenta—coarsely ground cornmeal cooked and cooled in a heavy pot and then turned over on a wooden board. The polenta would slide out in the shape of the pan. It was cut with a heavy cord, and each family member got a thick slice with a little red sauce poured over the top.

Other days, they would have a hearty soup made with vegetables from Gulio's garden. On baking day, Jenny would bake bread from coarsely ground wheat. It was not bleached but tan in color. As the bread baked, the aroma would fill the house, and the children clambered to the kitchen where the coal stove held the many loaves of bread. If the children were quiet and obedient, had washed themselves and combed their hair, and had finished their many chores, they were given a piece of warm bread with butter or jam. Sometimes there was no butter or jam, so they ate it plain—but still savored every morsel.

Johnny tells about a neighbor who put mayonnaise on her son's bread. Occasionally, when Johnny was playing there, he too would get a mayonnaise sandwich, which he thought was extra special.

The children soon learned that if they picked berries in the woods or apples from someone else's tree, they could sell them to the man at the company store and buy five cents' worth of bologna. Josephine loved Coca-Cola, and somehow she found money to buy it.

Children from Catholic homes were expected to be in Catholic school every weekday and in church on Sunday. If the priest found a child outside playing instead of in the classroom, he would take the child by the ear and march him to a seat in the church. Feeling embarrassed, the child would sit motionless, ear stinging, for the entire service. If any Catholic in town did not attend, Father Farri would go promptly after church to find out the reason for the parishioner's absents. Gulio was visited regularly by Father Farri, perhaps because of his absence from church, but also for wine—supposedly for Communion, but Gulio knew that his wine was being used for other purposes too. He would laugh and ask the priest, "Who is drinking all the wine?" He knew the priest favored his wine.

An Accident

On August 31, 1933, two farmers came into Ernest selling fruit and vegetables from their car. As the car began traveling down the hill, which was in the center of Ernest, four boys grabbed the bumper of the car to take a joyride. As the car approached the highway intersection, a large oil truck was making a turn in front of the car.

It is believed that the driver of the car was distracted momentarily, having just noticed the boys hanging onto his bumper. He apparently hit the gas pedal instead of the brake, and the car slammed into the oil truck, causing the boys' bodies to be thrown in front of and under the oil truck. Costantino Mari, age nine, and two of his friends were killed. Costantino's brother Eddie, who was seven years old, was thrown into a ditch. He was badly injured but not killed. The two farmers were also killed.

Everyone in town was scared and screaming. Mothers came running from every house wondering if it was their boy who was hurt or killed. This accident devastated the whole town. It was a terrible event for Jenny to experience. She was seven months pregnant with her seventh child, Connie, who was due in October.

This is Constantino, Johnny's oldest brother, who was killed at the age of nine along with two friends who were hanging onto the bumper of a moving car.

Mama's Sick

With the headaches she had been experiencing, the accident was more than Jenny could handle emotionally. At this time, doctors finally figured out that there was a blood clot on Jenny's brain, but they did not have the imaging equipment or the knowledge to remove it.

She was sent to Torrance State Mental Hospital. That was where the doctors sent women if they had any mental or emotional problems. There was mistreatment, shock treatments, and more, which were thought to be the answer at that time. Many, many women from that little town and neighboring towns were sent to Torrance suffering with depression, mood swings, or menopause. Jenny was kept there until Connie was born on October 30, 1933.

Some boys set an old wooden church on fire and rather than find the youngsters who did it, people accused Jenny. This made it embarrassing for the Mari children to play or talk to other children. At school, they were shunned and whispered about. It was like shame had come upon their home, and they didn't understand why.

"Oh No!"

One evening, Jenny and a neighbor lady were taking a walk down a country road. They passed a bar many of the resident men visited after work. As the two women were walking near a wooded area, suddenly a drunken man came out of the woods, grabbed Jenny, and dragged her deep into the woods. He raped her and then let her go. Jenny told Gulio what happened and who did it.

Gulio was beside himself with anger. He got his gun and went up the road toward the man's house, intending to shoot him. Before he got there, he changed his mind because he knew he would be sent to prison if he killed a man. That would not help his wife or family. Because of

Jenny's condition, the authorities would not believe her. Besides, this was a terrible embarrassment for Jenny.

Jenny became pregnant from the rape and gave birth to her last child in October 1939. The circumstances of this birth as well as the blood clot pressing on her brain were more than her body and mind could handle. She completely shut down mentally and was placed in Torrance State Mental Hospital for the remainder of her life. Jenny Mari died August 10, 1952, at age 47.

Gulio

By now, many immigrants had settled in Ernest, Pennsylvania, and made it their home. It had been thirty years since Gulio's arrival in the United States, and he still was not a citizen. His children were all citizens, of course, and it was time he became a citizen too.

A teacher at the elementary school was appointed to conduct citizenship classes. Gulio was among many who took them. He learned to read and write and speak English. He learned the history of America, the pledge of allegiance to the American flag, and the promise of loyalty to America. He changed his name to Julius Mari. Sometimes, he took seven-year-old Johnny to school, and the boy gave the teacher red roses picked from the rosebush that grew in the Maris' front yard. Julius Mari became a citizen of the United States on April 3, 1941. That was one proud day for Julius and his family.

Chapter 3

Julius was injured while working in the mine when a timber fell on his back. Months later, he was diagnosed with cancer of the intestines. He lived another two years, but by then he was in so much pain he could not stand it any longer.

ORIGINAL
TO BE GIVEN TO
THE PERSON NATURALIZED

Petition No. 4562

No. 4901472

UNITED STATES OF AMERICA

DECLARATION OF NATURALIZATION

Description of holder: Age 55 years; sex Male; color White; complexion Fair; color of eyes Gray; color of hair Gray; height 5 feet, 4 inches; visible distinguishing marks None; Former nationality Italy; Married.

I certify that the description above given is true, and that the photograph affixed hereto is a likeness of me.

Giulino Mari

Seal

Commonwealth of Pa. }
County of Indiana. } ss:

Be it known that Julius Mari

Ernest, Pa.
Now residing at Indiana, Pa.

having petitioned to be admitted a citizen of the United States of America, and at a term of the Common Pleas Court of Indiana County held pursuant to law at Indiana, Pa. on April 3, 19

A. B. Ansley, Clerk.

A. B. Ansley,
Clerk of the Common Pleas, Court.

By Leonard Howard Deputy Clerk.

April
Forty one
and
Sixty fifth

3rd

In March of 1942, Julius told a neighbor who was a county commissioner that he didn't have long to live and needed to make plans for the care of his children. She wrote down his requests for their care. He had money designated for the funeral and burial of himself and Jenny. He also had a few dollars saved, and he designated the amount for each of his children.

"No, Papa, No!"

On March 24, 1942, Julius ate dinner with his children and then went to his bedroom. A few moments later he lovingly said, *"Arrivederci la figligis,"* which in Italian meant, "Good-bye my daughters." The girls were washing the dishes.

One daughter turned to him, asking, "Where are you going, Papa?" Without answering, he stepped outside the kitchen door, and with one shot to his temple he fell. The girls rushed to the door to find their father bleeding to death where he fell back onto the kitchen floor. Little six-year-old Tommy picked up his father's head and cried, "Oh Daddy, Daddy, Daddy!"

Johnny was in the woods playing. He heard the shot and wondered where it had come from. His friend said, "It sounded like it came from your house." They both ran to see and were horrified to find it was Johnny's dad.

A doctor and a priest were called. When the priest arrived, he cried, "Oh Julius, Julius, why have you done this? You have committed your soul to hell!"

What a thing to say in the presence of children! What a lasting nightmare this was for them. First their mother got sick and was taken away, never to return home. Then their father got hurt, then sick, and now he was dead. Why? What would happen to them now? Who would take care of them? Why did both parents have to leave them? As if this was not enough, shame was cast on Julius for committing suicide.

The family was not permitted to have a funeral in the Catholic Church. It was also declared that Julius could not be buried in the Catholic cemetery because of the mortal sin the Church said he had committed. Later, it was decided he could be buried in the lower part of the cemetery "that had not been blessed." Instead of comforting the children and explaining that their father did this because he was out of his mind with pain, the priest could only say that suicide was an unforgivable sin, and shame and condemnation was cast upon their father. The priest did not think about the devastating effect this would have on Julius's precious children.

The county welfare agency stepped in and followed some of the father's wishes. He wanted the Catholic Church to find a home where his children would all be together. The three oldest children—Josephine, age twenty; Eddie, almost eighteen; and Rose Marie, age sixteen—had to fend for themselves. Josephine was married and expecting a baby. Eddie had quit school, and as soon as he was old enough, he joined the army. Rose Marie ran away with a girlfriend to another state so she would not be taken to an orphanage.

Where Is Home Now?

The others were taken to St. Anthony's Orphanage in Pittsburgh. These children were taken away without counseling or time to grieve. They were expected to keep their chins up, and they were told, "Big boys don't cry." People really believed if they hurried and changed the environment, the children would forget their unhappy past and get on with their lives.

In fact, without realizing it, the children just put their grief on hold. They lost their self-esteem and self-worth. They did not see themselves worthy of life or happiness. They were terribly confused about their parents. Should they defend their parents for the love they had for them or condemn them, as the church was doing?

All they knew was that they were really angry at their mother and father for leaving them orphans without family or home. Oh, how it tore at their hearts to watch as authorities came and took their siblings away. Grown-ups told the children that they should try to accept the fact that it was one of those things that just happens. But it didn't "just happen" to anyone else, only the Maris. Why, why did all this have to happen to them?

It didn't matter, because there was no one to talk to about anger or sadness or being lonely for siblings or parents or home. It seemed to the children that there was no one in the whole world who cared if they lived or died. These feelings caused much fear, anxiety, and anger to well up in the children.

Discipline at St. Anthony's was very harsh, often to the point of abuse—but then abuse was not considered harmful at that time. The nuns pulled the children's ears or lifted their skirts to kick their behinds for any reason, and the children were often slapped. They were made to scrub the floor with a toothbrush and clean toilets with their bare hands. Some of the children were placed in St. Paul's orphanage in Pittsburgh for a while, which was run very similarly.

One day, Johnny, wishing for his dad's polenta, grumbled under his breath about his dinner, and he said a swear word. The priest was within hearing distance. He took Johnny to the kitchen, poured a handful of pepper, and threw it down Johnny's throat. It nearly killed him. Johnny didn't think he would ever be able to stop choking or gagging, or regain his breathing.

The priest thought he had cured Johnny of swearing, but instead he caused Johnny to hate the priest, the nuns, and the church. It was a priest who had condemned his father to hell, and a priest who nearly killed him. Johnny continued to be angry inside. Where was this loving God everyone talked about?

Julia had a different experience. She was an adorable child—timid, quiet, and obedient. The nuns lavished attention on her. They talked sweetly to her, brushed her long dark hair, and told her how beautiful she was. She loved the nuns, the priest, and the Church. She gave some thought to becoming a nun herself. She enjoyed her stay at the orphanage and had fond memories of it, even as an adult. Julia loved and honored the Church her entire life. But she never got over the heartache and misery of losing her home, her parents, and her siblings.

There were three family members in Detroit who felt they could each take a child to raise rather than allow all these children to be raised in an orphanage. Julia and Connie were sent to live with those families. One family member was also willing to take Tommy.

This did not sit well with Josephine, the eldest daughter, who believed she was acting on her father's wishes that the children be raised together. She contacted the family in Detroit and demanded the children be brought back to their home in Ernest immediately, which they were. She went to the orphanages where her other siblings were and took them home without permission. Josephine could have been charged with kidnapping, but authorities felt she was acting out her father's wishes and attempting to protect her younger siblings.

However, after an investigation, authorities found that Josephine was not able financially, emotionally, or physically to raise these children. Her home was not a stable environment. Josephine's husband had left her while she was pregnant. She had her baby to care for and support. She had very little income and was not able to work. The child welfare agency did not feel this was a home in which to place six more children. It was impossible to put them all in the Williard Home, a county-supported home for orphaned and disadvantaged children that housed forty to fifty children at a time, so the three youngest children—Connie, Tommy, and Freddie—were permitted to stay with their sister Josephine for a while.

Josephine's income was subsidized, but still there was very little to eat at times. Later, Connie and Tommy were removed and taken to St. Paul's

Catholic Orphanage in Pittsburgh. Freddie, the youngest, went to live with his sister Rose Marie in New Jersey.

When they were a little older, they were all placed in the Williard Home.

Josephine Mari Yuckenburg   Joe & Rose Marie Gauteri

Constance Mari

Julia Mari Broskin

Children's Industrial Home, Eleventh St.

Susan Hauxhurts Williard

SUE WILLIARD . . . mother to many

Area Honored Mrs. Williard

Prominent among the out-standing women of Indiana was Mrs. Sue Williard who founded and served as overseer of the Girls' Industrial Home in Indiana.

This institution was established in Indiana in 1894 under the cares of the Children's Aid Society of Western Pennsylvania. The home was first considered at a meeting of that Society in Oil City. Three local units were... part because of the character and personality of Mrs. Williard the Society chose Indiana.

After the Children's Aid Society purchased the Major McFarland home at Eleventh and Washington Streets, Mrs. Williard was placed in charge. The property, now Washington House and used as a small dormitory by Indiana University of Pennsylvania, originally cost $5,000 and included one acre of ground. Mrs. Williard's direction, the property was soon improved and was valued in 1913 at $15,600.

The building accommodated sixteen girls who were given family training and home life. A separate building adjoining the main structure served the purpose of a schoolhouse. The society employed a matron and a teacher. A Miss Bratton served as matron for several decades in the period from 1903 on.

The object of the Girls' Industrial Home was to train girls in housekeeping, give them a good school education, and then place them in good homes.

Girls were admitted to the home between the ages of eight and sixteen. It is believed that during the period 1893 to 1933 a total of about 825 girls were trained at the Girls' Industrial School and placed in homes. The girls learned housekeeping, sewing, gardening, and did all the housework of the institution under the supervision of the matron.

During the entire existence of the Girl's Industrial School at the Eleventh St. location, Mrs. Williard and a committee of three Indiana women belonging to the Children's Aid Society formed the directing group.

County authorities, of course, had an interest in a children's homes. A state regulation during the earlier decades of this century prohibited such homes from being established on the same property as the County home.

Indiana County authorities wished to use the Elmer Campbell home adjacent to the Indiana County Home for a children's home but were impeded in this development by the existing state regulation.

Mrs. Sue Williard went to Harrisburg, fought the regulation, and gained state permission for the Indiana County Commissioners to use the former Campbell place as a child... In 1921 a home was set up there and called the Williard Home in honor of Mrs. Williard. The Williard Home served admirably for many years until 1965 as a county establishment to care for underprivileged children, orphans, and youngsters from broken homes.

By 1965 the Commissioners found that newer "foster home" programs were more effective in caring for needy children and the Williard Home as a... children's home was abandoned. The building, however, is being used for other worthy county purposes including providing badly needed office space.

Mrs. Williard's interest in working with children was life-long, but after her husband's death in 1925, she decided to devote her life to good works in the town and county.

She was literally the mother to scores of homeless and indigent girls in the Western Pennsylvania area. Her influence helped instill hope and better living in many young lives.

Mrs. Williard spared neither personal time nor expense in developing good work among unfortunate children.

Mrs. Sue Williard, affectionately called "Aunty Sue" by several generations of Indianians was born at Babylon, Long Island, N.Y., the daughter of Solomon and Ann Jackson Hawxhurst, on Jan. 10, 1843.

She married Robert Williard at the "Old Mill" south of Indiana (along Indian Springs Road) in 1862.

For a number of years, Mr. Williard, born July 20, 1838, was engaged in the painting and mill business then located on the corner of Philadelphia and Tenth Streets.

After his death on N... 1885, Mrs. Williard con... the business herself for five years, before selling firm to Getty and Carnath.

Mrs. Williard continued... residence at 557 Philadelphia... until her death on July 6,... During the long lifetime... Children's Aid Society of... sylvania, the Girls' Ind... School of Indiana, W... House, the First Presby... Church, and a myriad of other o... nizations for good, and ins... ble individuals received... comfort and support from... Williard.

This picture was taken in 1943 with thirty-four children present. Mrs. Rowley is holding the small baby. Standing with a bow tie is Mr. Rowley. Beside him is his son Bud, wearing white shirt and tie. Our dear grandma Dowdy is beside Mrs. Rowley.

Willard Home School students posed with teacher Miss Gemmell for this 1944 photo shared by Betty Airgood Lydick of Indiana, fifth from right in the second row. The class includes, from left in the front row, Dennis Bathurst, Ruthann Skinner, Sally Bathurst, (unidentified), Martha Jane Simpson, Shirley Airgood, Berniece Fairley, David DeHaven and Dick Leasure. In the second row: Jimmy Allison, Annabel Marsh, Bobby Fairley, Ed Shaw, Lillian Leasure, Charles Marsh, Betty Airgood, Harry Shaw, Bob Austin, Betty Miller and Louise Shields. Third row: Mary Ann Marshall, (unidentified), David Hodge, (unidentified), Joe Gobor, Sarah Jane Kanouff, LeRoy Ewing, Don Myers, Freddie Baxter, Leonard Lowman and Miss Gemmell.

This picture was taken at a Christmas party at the Williard Home in 1952. Standing: (left to right) David Hodge, brother of Patty Hodge, sitting behind the boys, holding Linda Valuchuck. The four other boys are Arthur Robinson, Ward Zeigler, Walter Moreau, and Earl Steel. Sitting in front of the boys is Janet Valuchuck, sister of Linda Valuchuck.

Easter Bunny's Helpers Visit Willard Home Children Sunday

The Easter Bunny couldn't make it to the Willard Home this year, so he sent his special helpers, the 40 et 8, Indiana Voiture 798, to care for the youngsters at the local institution.

Sunday afternoon, nine of these helpers visited the home and presented each youngster with an Easter basket. The kids were also treated to ice cream and cake.

During the afternoon, all the kids were given rides on the 40 et 8 locomotive which included a trip through Indiana.

A report in the Gazette said that some of the kids were up at dawn waiting to see the Bunny's helpers.

28

This picture was taken in 1958 at the Williard Home. People I know:
Mrs. Merrill
Mr. Merlo: Merlo Beer Distributing
First row: Linda Valuchuck
Two boys younger Valuchuck
Boy, Janet Valuchuck
Third row-center: Lucy Koffman

The Williard Home orphanage was for orphaned, disadvantaged, neglected, or abused children. It was built adjacent to the county home. In the 1960s, the Williard Home was closed and children were placed in foster care. The building was used for offices while the new courthouse was being built. Shortly after, it burned down. A nursing home was built in its place.

Long before the Williard Home was built, the county home was erected for the poor elderly folks in Indiana County. It is privately owned and is called the Rose Haven. It is no longer for the needy and poor.

Soon after the three aunts brought the girls back to Ernest to their sister, the child welfare agency took four of the children and placed them in the Williard Home. This picture was taken when Josephine visited her siblings. Freddie the youngest child was living with Josephine but visiting his siblings at the Williard Home.

During the years that the Mari children were in the Williard Home, they did not consider it anything like home. They were placed there so they would all be together, but they were separated most of the time, not knowing where their siblings were or how they were doing.

The Matrons

Johnny was very fond of the matron, Mrs. Rowley, and tried his best to be good and not fight or get into trouble. That was hard, since there were so many kids and workers there to get along with. He found himself sitting behind the dining room door so many times and wishing he could be outdoors playing ball.

One day, Mrs. Rowley called Johnny into the office and told him she had to make a very important decision. She was to pick a Catholic boy who would like to live at Boys Town. He would be well cared for, receive a good education, and be given his choice of a trade school or college. Since Johnny was fearful and untrusting of the priests and the Church, and since his sister insisted the children be together, Mrs. Rowley chose another boy to go to Boys Town. Johnny often wondered how different his life might have been had he been chosen.

In 1949, a change came about. Mrs. Rowley became very ill, and a new matron, Mrs. Dorothy Merrill, and her husband, George, were put in charge of the Williard Home. Mrs. Merrill made some nice changes for the children. The tin plates were replaced with yellow plastic plates and bowls. New plastic glasses were purchased, but the old brown mugs remained. Also remaining was the physical abuse that had become common in the Williard Home. The children were whipped for running away, not doing an assigned job, or "telling a lie"—even when it was the truth.

When Tommy was sixteen years old, he saw a black boy seducing a white girl (the matron's daughter) in the coal bin. He told the matron what her daughter was doing after he was caught doing the same thing to one of the girls. It was a story the matron could not believe, and so Tommy was punished. Later, the story was proven true. Too bad the matron couldn't see trouble ahead, because her daughter ended up with three black children and died an early death of liver disease. The matron ended up having to raise her three grandchildren.

In fact, the children in the Williard Home were punished for most anything. Right after dinner, George would call three or four boys to stand in front of everyone. Using a very thick wooden paddle with holes in it, George would then spank the boys until they screamed with pain. It was horrible to watch. When George was finished spanking the boys, he would turn to the other children and say, "Take that for a lesson because if you disobey, that is what you will get."

George bragged to some of his friends that he had his own harem at the Williard Home. Rules didn't apply to him. He just enforced some of them.

The state provided a huge ring of butter and cheese for the children. The county raised many chickens, and eggs were also provided. George stole a lot of the eggs, cheese, and butter and sold it. He was caught and went to prison. I don't know how long he had to serve.

There was a so-called "fine Christian man" who would drive children to Sunday school. He then began taking one or two boys out for the day. It was not until years later that it was discovered that he was sexually assaulting those boys. Patty's brother was one of them. The man apparently threatened them so they wouldn't tell. By the time the authorities knew about this, it was too late. Too many years had gone by, and nothing was ever done about it.

Foster Homes

Work farms were found for as many teens as possible. Nobody wanted a troubled teen unless he or she could work and work hard. The farmer got free hands to help with the plowing, planting, and harvesting of crops as well as milking cows and cleaning the barn, mowing the grass, chopping the wood, and many other farm chores. It was work from early morning until dark. The boys and girls were not given praise or allowance, but the farmer was given a monthly check. After harvest time, the teen was almost always returned to the orphanage.

Foster parents were told not to show the child affection or make promises because this was a temporary home. Children were not to get the impression they were loved, for what if the biological parents got their children back or the foster parents changed their minds and were not able to care for the child or teen any longer? So most foster homes did nothing for the child's self-confidence or self-esteem. Many children took last place and were mistreated by the biological children of that home.

Often a foster parent, relative, or family friend sexually or emotionally abused the child in foster care. This brought on misbehavior and angry attitudes. At the first sign of misbehavior, children were taken back to the Williard Home without counseling and often led to believe that they were bad boys and girls who didn't appreciate this "Christian family" giving them a home.

As teenagers, both Johnny and Julia were placed in separate work farms several miles from one another. If either had any spare time, he or she would walk the many miles to visit the other. How they longed to be a family once again.

Johnny hated farming, so he was returned to the Williard Home—after the harvest. The following year, he was put on another work farm. He was helping cut the hay and get it into the barn. It was extremely hot, and Johnny became very ill and had a high fever. They called it "hay fever," so he was sent back to the Williard Home. A sick kid was no use to a farmer.

Johnny knew he would have to leave the Williard Home and be on his own when he turned eighteen years old. He didn't know what to do or where to go, so instead of going into his senior year of high school, he joined the army. He had heard about the Korean War but figured it would be over by the time he finished basic training. He soon discovered that he had jumped out of the frying pan into the fire.

Chapter 4

On July 6, 1950, Johnny joined the army. After twelve weeks of basic training at Fort Knox, Kentucky, he was shipped out to a post in Japan, but only temporarily. When the troops arrived in Japan, they were loaded onto a ship headed for Korea. They landed by LST (a landing aircraft) in Inchon.

This is Johnny in Korea.
He was a tank gunner.
He still looks like a young boy.

This is Johnny as staff sergeant,
stationed in France with the
Korean experience behind him.

It was October 15, 1950—a very cold and rainy day. The soldiers had not been given winter clothing or warm heavy boots. They were given two blankets and told to sleep on the ground. In the morning, Johnny was assigned to the 25th Recon Company and loaded on a train with straw on the floor for hauling cattle. The trip was cold and nasty.

They arrived at the capital city of North Korea, called Pyongyang. From there they were transported by truck to the 25th Recon Company headquarters near Ipsock. Johnny was cold and tired, wishing for a warm safe bed to sleep in. He longed for a hot meal, a hot bath, and dry clean clothes. If only he'd stayed in the orphanage. But there was no turning back now.

He awoke one morning hemorrhaging from a frostbitten nose. Johnny was sent to the medics, treated, and sent back into battle. He had tapeworms from the cold, partially cooked sea rations. He lost a lot of weight and became quite ill. Again, Johnny was sent to the medics, who gave him medication. After he had passed twenty-one tapeworms, he was sent back into battle. He lost a good part of his hearing from the huge submachine gun he fired from the army tank.

More than anything, Johnny was lonely and homesick. But homesick for what? He had no home to return home to. Patty, a girl from the Williard Home, had written to him and sent cookies. Even though the cookies were too hard to eat, he knew he must remember to thank her for her kindness when he returned to the states.

One day as he and another soldier were returning to their tank with their lunch in hand, the other soldier stepped on a land mine, which blew his foot off. Flesh and blood sprayed up all over Johnny. The soldier was screaming for Johnny to help him.

The commanding officer was nearby and ordered Johnny not to move or lift a foot; he said they would get both men out of there. With bayonet in hand, Francis Young searched underground for any other land mines and removed the men without further injury. Johnny was forever grateful to Francis for saving his life that day.

The other soldier, whose name was Vernon Utter, was immediately transferred to a hospital for treatment and rehabilitation. Johnny never heard from or saw Vernon again.

Johnny saw refugees lying dead beside the road for miles, and babies still strapped to their mothers' backs frozen to death. He wondered if there really was a God—a caring, loving God. Why would He allow this to happen to these people? Somehow, he believed there was a God, but wondered where He was when a person needed Him the most.

There were little children lost or abandoned by their parents begging for food. Johnny shared many of his sea rations with these children. He learned to speak a little of their language and listened as the children sang their little songs to the soldiers in thanks for food they shared.

"Ah-dee-da, ah-dee-da, ah-da-de-da … Ah-dee-da ah-dee-da ah-da-de-oh." They were sweet children, homeless and hungry, and yet so grateful for a little bit to eat.

This is John Mari leaning on the tank with Vernon Utter.
Vernon was from South Dakota and was the soldier who
got his foot blown off by the land mine

Johnny's tank got destroyed by a land mine in 1950

Jenny

Johnny served a year in Korea. After that, he was sent home for a furlough and was then stationed at Camp Kilmore, New Jersey. He went to his commanding officer and asked to be shipped overseas. Within a few days, he was told to prepare to leave for France. Within a day of receiving his orders, he was called to the commanding officer's office, where he was told that his mother had died. It was August 10, 1952.

Johnny's sister Rose Marie and her husband, Joe, who lived in New Jersey, came to get him to take him to their mother's funeral in Indiana, Pennsylvania. On the way to Indiana, they told him that just before Jenny died, the blood clot broke loose from her brain. Her mind was clear, but she was confused as to why she was in the hospital.

She spoke to a nurse, and the nurse recorded everything Jenny said. She named each one of her children and her husband. By then, the blood clot had reached her heart; it caused a heart attack, and she died. The cause of death was the blood clot that had caused her mental illness. The poor woman never had a chance to live a happy, good life.

Private Thomas M. Mari taking his basic training
with (A) Battery, 675th Field Artillery
of the famous 11th Airborne Division,
Fort Campbell, Kentucky.

Private Thomas M. Mari entered the service on
June 4, 1953. He became a qualified parachutist,
having completed the three-week airborne
school at Fort Benning, Georgia on December 8, 1953.

Discharge

After his mother's funeral, Johnny returned to base and immediately
prepared to go to France. He was sent there to work in construction,
building ammunition decks in case of another war. The French people
did not trust the US government, the army, or Americans. They put
up signs that said, "Americans, Go Home." Johnny wasn't wanted or
welcomed there at all. Was there any place he was welcome?

Soon Johnny would be discharged. Who would he go home to? Was
there anyone to welcome him home? Johnny decided to relax, have
some fun, and make the most of the time he had left in the army. He
became buddies with some of the guys and began touring the cities and
enjoying himself.

Johnny served three years in the army and was honorably discharged in 1953. Just as he was being released, he saw a group of new recruits coming on base. As they passed in the hall, he saw a familiar face. It was his younger brother Tommy! They greeted each other with surprise and a hug. Johnny wished Tommy good health and safety. As they parted, Johnny had a sad feeling in his heart. Here was another brother jumping out of the frying pan into the fire of war. Had he known his brother's intention, he would have advised Tommy to stay put and finish school. It was too late now, though. Tommy had already enlisted and was now in the army.

Home Again

Seeing that there were no people, bands, or confetti to welcome him or the hundreds of other soldiers coming home, Johnny realized he was truly alone with no place to call home. A buddy who he knew from high school, Jimmy Hicks, had been in his same unit, but Johnny was discharged before him. Jimmy said, "Johnny, you go to my parents' home and stay with them until you know where to go." So Johnny went to Jimmy's home and stayed there until he was able to contact his sister Josephine.

Josephine had divorced her first husband and married Harry Yuckenburg, and they had two children besides Judy, her daughter from her first marriage. She had moved and her last name had changed. It took a while for Johnny to realize why it was taking so long to find his sister, but finally they were reunited and he moved into her home.

While he was staying with Josephine and her family, he had terrible nightmares. One night he barricaded her living room by stacking all the furniture up against the door. His sister didn't understand and didn't appreciate what she found the following morning. Her husband understood perfectly, having been in the war himself.

Johnny recognized that staying with his sister was causing a problem, so he only stayed a couple of weeks. His goal was to find a job. He applied at the Sharon Steel Company in Sharon, Pennsylvania. He was hired, but it was so noisy with loud crashing and banging that it shattered Johnny's nerves. He just couldn't take the noise, so he quit and began looking for another job.

Johnny asked Josephine about the others in the family—where did they live, were they married, did they have children? Josephine went through the list of siblings. Ed had married Emma, an Italian girl; they had a little boy named Frankie and they lived in Dearborn Heights, Michigan. Rose Marie and Joe Gauteri, Johnny knew about from their mother's funeral. Julia had married Joe Broskin; they had two sons named Joey and Ronnie, and they lived in Pittsburgh. Connie had married Mead Shank, and they had several children. Tommy was in the army, and Freddie, their youngest brother, was still in the Williard Home.

Nearly all of his siblings were getting on with their lives, and Johnny felt it was time for him to do the same. Where would he start? Where would he live? Where would he get a job?

Johnny left his sister's home in Sharon and went to Michigan to visit Ed. His brother told him that the Detroit Edison Power Company, where he worked, was hiring. It was in 1953 that Johnny put in his application at Edison, and he was hired as a laborer digging ditches, busting concrete, and other doing other laborious jobs.

Patty

It was in the spring of 1954 that Patty asked Johnny to the prom. He was delighted by the invitation, and they had a wonderful time. That year, Patty graduated from high school, and it was time for her to leave the Willard Home. She rented a room in town and got a job as a waitress in a restaurant.

December 10, 1954, was Patty's nineteenth birthday. Johnny had gotten a car and arrived at Patty's door at ten in the morning. He asked Patty if she would marry him, and of course she said yes. They went shopping that day, and Johnny bought Patty a small but beautiful diamond ring. They set their wedding date for August 22, 1955. Johnny went back to Michigan to work, and Patty stayed in Indiana, Pennsylvania, to do the same.

At Christmas, they were both invited to Johnny's sister Julia's home in Pittsburgh. When Johnny came to pick Patty up, she had a surprise for him. She was packed ready to move to Michigan. Johnny was truly surprised, and he asked, "Where will you live until we get married?"

Patty replied, "I'll rent a room just like I did here."

Johnny had brought his brother Ed with him. Johnny turned to Ed and asked, "Could Patty stay with you and Emma until we can find her a room and a job?"

Ed answered, "Sure she can."

The day after Christmas, the three of them left for Michigan. Patty stayed with Ed and Emma for about a week until she found a room and a job.

This is Edward Mari and his wife, Emma.
They lived for many years in Dearborn Heights, Michigan.
They had one son, Frank. Frank and his wife, Constance,
had two sons, Frank Jr. and Nicolas.
Frank Sr. is a family physician, and both his sons are now attorneys

Patty worked for Bell Telephone in the cafeteria until a friend told her about a job opening at a title company in Detroit, where she worked. Patty got a room in Dearborn and a job at the title company and worked there from January until August. Johnny and Patty were married as planned on August 22, 1955, in Indiana, Pennsylvania. Johnny bought a brand-new mobile home, and after a short honeymoon they settled down, hoping to live happily ever after.

Johnny and Patty were married on August 22, 1955
at the Lutheran Church in Indiana, Pennsylvania.

Part II

Chapter 5

Jesse Hodge was a strapping young boy. He was tanned and calloused from the hard work he did on his father's farm. It was adjacent to the Thompson farm, where Anna Thompson helped her parents as they worked together in the fields, milking the cows, cleaning the barn, feeding the many chickens, and gathering eggs. She cooked and cleaned with her mother and helped care for her younger siblings. Jesse thought of Anna as just a beanpole in pigtails—and of course, the kid from a neighboring farm.

One day Jesse saw Anna as she brought her father a lunch basket. She was no longer that scrawny little girl but a beautiful young woman. What a charm she was. Her hair was long, and it bounced and glittered in the sun as she walked.

As the summer passed, he watched for her and listened to her laughter. She always seemed so full of joy. How she adored her father. Every day she brought a red-checked tablecloth, laid it out on the ground under a shade tree, and set a lunch for two. Jesse could hear her chatter and laughter in the distance. Sometimes she would sing, and her voice was so sweet it gave him goose bumps.

Jesse was determined to ask Anna to the barn dance that following week. He did, and she happily accepted. Jesse bid the highest price on the picnic lunch packed in that same wicker basket that was brought by Anna to the field each day.

As time and parents allowed, Jesse and Anna spent many an hour together, walking talking, singing, and attending church activities.

Jesse tried courting other girls and Anna courted other fellows, but Jesse knew it was Anna he loved. There was never another girl who touched his heart like Anna. When Jesse was twenty-two and Anna was nineteen, they married. They built a small house on the land between their parents' homes so they could continue to farm the land, and they did. They wanted many children, and each year Anna was pregnant with another baby. With each baby, she hoped her wish would be granted and she would have a girl.

Twelve children were born to Jesse and Anna: eleven boys and just one girl. It was quite a disappointment for Anna that she didn't have more girls, but Jesse swelled with pride each time he held another newborn son. Jesse came from a strong heritage of educated men and teachers. Their work was published and taught all over America as well as abroad. Others in his family had succeeded in business and farming. Jesse loved farming but dreamed that someday he too would see some of his sons in the ministry, while others carried on with the farming of this land.

Warren Hodge

Warren Clarence Hodge was one of the sons born to Jesse and Anna. He was born May 6, 1886. He grew up loving the land and farming, and he was determined to carry on the care and ownership of the Hodge and Thompson farms. But when he was eighteen years old, World War I broke out. Men were needed to serve. His buddies had all enlisted, and he knew he must go and serve his country. He didn't want his younger brothers to have to go to war. So he enlisted, bid his family good-bye, and left for Europe.

Warren was stationed in Germany when he met an American army nurse working in a hospital there. They fell in love and were married in Germany. She continued her work there until she was pregnant, and then she returned to her parents' home in the states to have her baby. She had a son and called him Ellsworth Hodge. Since nurses were needed so badly in Germany, she left the baby with her parents and returned to Germany, to Warren, to the war … and to a horrible disease.

Six months after her return to Germany, she was stricken with the Black Plague that was so prevalent and so contagious. It had taken the lives of hundreds of thousands of civilians, children, soldiers, and medical personal. Little children sang a song in the streets called "Ring Around the Rosie." The people could hear them sing: "Ring around the rosie, a pocket full of posies. Ashes, ashes, we all fall down." Their play indicated the death of so many of their loved ones. As people circled the dying person, they would lay flowers on the body. Then they rubbed their own bodies in ashes and watched as so many more fell to their death. It was a horrible, horrible disease.

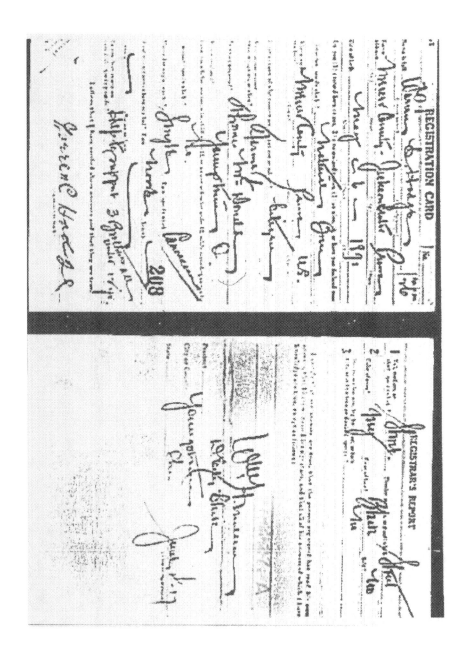

The Black Plague took this young woman's life, leaving behind a young grieving husband, a child who would never know his mother, and loving grieving parents. Warren grieved the death of his wife, who to him was still a bride. They'd had so little time together, and now she was gone. Warren returned home with his wife's body to be buried in her family cemetery.

Since the baby had lived with his grandparents since birth and did not know Warren was his dad, the grandparents felt it was best for them to raise the boy. It was their desire that after Warren returned from the war, the child should continue living with them, and Warren should not visit or interfere with his son's life. Warren did as he was requested and did not interfere, but he kept his two loves in his heart. He watched from afar as his son grew up.

All through his time in the service, Warren strived to save every penny he could. He also received money from his wife's death benefit. His wife's parents requested that he keep the death benefit in return for letting them raise their grandson.

After the war, when Warren was discharged, he decided to get on with his life and get back to farming. It was a time in history when farmers were encouraged to clear the land and establish homesteads. Warren was able to clear land for four small farms and hire farmhands to live there and tend the farms for him. One was a cattle farm, another was a vegetable farm, and the other two were grain farms. He was proud of how they were progressing, and at last he felt his dream of being a farmer finally was coming true.

A New Life with a New Wife

Warren met the Albert Johnston family of Glen Campbell, Pennsylvania. Albert Allen Johnston was born in 1880 in Banks Township, Pennsylvania. His wife, Emma Golden Pennington, was born on February 24, 1878, and raised in Glen Campbell. Albert was nicked named "Bert" or "Pup." Albert and Emma had five children: Enid Mila, born December 20, 1903; Albert John, born December 6, 1906; Mary, born in 1908; Golden, born September 8, 1910; and Robert, born in April, 1914.

Albert traveled a lot for his work and was rarely home, but when he was, there was constant conflict because of his heavy drinking. This left the children concerned about their future. They knew their mother was not well, and it worried them when they felt their father was abusive to their mother both verbally and physically. Emma died on May 24, 1914; the cause of her death was not recorded. She was thirty-six years old, and it was just a month after her son Robert was born. Enid Mila was ten at the time, Albert John was eight, and Golden was five. After Emma's death, the children were cared for mostly by relatives and neighbors.

When Mila was yet a teen, she was noticed by every man in town, and Warren was no exception. He saw how beautiful she was and how much she needed to have someone to truly care for her. After a very short courtship, Warren realized he was very much in love with Mila and wanted to make her happy. Mila and Warren were married in 1920, when Mila was just sixteen years old.

The farms were beginning to produce nicely, and Warren felt comfortable with the income they were providing. He had a beautiful home built for himself and Mila. He hired a housekeeper to clean and cook. All he asked of Mila was to be beautiful for him, and she did that. When Warren came home in the evening, she was bathed and dressed to please him.

Within the first year of marriage, Mila was pregnant with twins. It was a very difficult pregnancy, and the babies were born premature. Both babies died. The following year, 1922, Mila gave birth to a son, William; they called him Bill. In 1923, Nancy Elizabeth, who was called Betty, was born. Bertha was born in 1925. In 1927, Richard was born, and in 1929, Dorothy was born.

Chapter 6

Life hands out some pretty hard turns, and this family had its share. In 1929, the Depression hit—and it hit the Hodge family hard. In 1931, while pregnant with Ruby, Mila was struck by a car and injured so gravely she was not expected to live. She was hospitalized for months, and the bills quickly drained Warren of all income. He lost all four farms.

Ruby was born on December 19, 1931. She was brought home to the other children while Mila remained hospitalized. The children were cared for by a housekeeper until Warren was no longer able to pay her. Relatives, friends, and neighbors helped as best they could. Warren had to go away from home and often out of state to look for work. As often as he could, he would send money for the children.

He had no car, so he could only get home when someone else was going his direction. He had planted a garden so that whoever was caring for the children would have food while he was away. The housekeeper used everything out of the garden, and others who also needed food perhaps helped themselves to the garden until there was nothing left. One day there was one egg in the house and very little else. Betty, being about seven, cooked the egg and shared it with one of her sisters. She was severely punished for eating the egg.

Betty learned how to beg and scrounge for the needs of her family. She would go to the railroad tracks where coal cars passed each day. The cars were piled high with coal, and as they bumped and rolled down the tracks, the coal would fall off and roll on the ground. Betty was always there to get a bucket or two. She would also pick apples from trees and take them home for her siblings.

One day, when she was about ten years old, Betty saw a group of highway workers sitting under a tree eating lunch. She stood behind a tree watching the men eat, thinking that they would not see her. The men saw the little girl and knew she had to be hungry. Each shared a portion of his lunch with her. She ran home delighted that she had enough food to feed her whole family. Each day she went back to where the men ate lunch, and each day they brought her more food.

There was a tavern not far from the house, and at night it was quite busy and noisy. Betty would go to the tavern and pound on the door. Someone would come to the door and, seeing a child, would tell her to go home and slam the door. But Betty would go back and continue to pound on the door until someone threw coins out at her and threatened to call the police. She would go home satisfied, knowing she could buy some eggs or meat; she and her siblings would have food for at least another day.

Good-bye Dorothy

One day a horse-drawn wagon pulled up by the house. A young couple got down from the wagon and inquired if the housekeeper had anything to trade for fresh vegetables: "Flour, sugar, coffee, or any staple?"

The housekeeper replied, "I don't have anything here but kids, and they are all hungry. You can have any one of them you choose if you can give me a large bag of potatoes."

The couple looked at each other and looked around. They saw a tiny girl of about three hiding in the ditch. That tiny girl was Dorothy, and she was traded for a fifty-pound bag of potatoes. The couple wrote down the child's father's name and address but never gave the housekeeper theirs, claiming they traveled a lot and had no permanent address. The housekeeper knew that in the summer months, they farmed in

Pennsylvania. They did not tell her that in the winter, they worked the carnival all the way to Florida. Warren searched for Dorothy the rest of his life but never found her.

Each time Warren went away, when he returned home, one more child would be gone. Sometimes it was a housekeeper who gave a child away, and sometimes it was Mila, the children's own mother. She simply couldn't cope with problems, especially hungry children.

The Stoups

One of the men working on the highway came to the Hodge home. His name was Howard Stoup. He told the housekeeper who he was and offered to take Betty to raise. He promised to provide her with food, clothing, an education, and medical care. Howard needed a girl to help care for his ailing wife, Edith, who had diabetes and often had fainting spells.

Betty went to live with the Stoups, and she soon found herself doing more and more work on the farm. She thought constantly about her baby sister, Ruby, who was three at the time. Betty worried that she was not getting the care she needed or enough to eat. Betty cried and begged the Stoups to let Ruby come and live there too. She promised she would take care of the little girl.

The Stoups went back to the Hodge home and got Ruby and took her to their home. Instead of a sister relationship between Betty and Ruby, however, there was more like a parent-child relationship. Betty took responsibility for raising Ruby. This was hard for both girls, since Betty was still a child herself.

Some Amish friends of the Stoups took Bertha to live with them. It was not so much the work Bertha minded as the Amish rules. When she finished eighth grade, Bertha so wanted to go on to high school, but this was not permitted. Amish children were not permitted to go any further than the eighth grade.

Bertha felt she had no choice but to leave this family and find a place to live that would permit her to go to high school. She ran away and found a Jewish family in town she could stay with. She agreed to care for their children and help with chores. In return, this family not only let Bertha finish high school but college too. She worked in a luggage company to pay for college.

Bill and Richard seemed to do okay at home. They never had much, but without the girls at home, there was more to eat, and they got along with what they had. Mila was very fond of the boys and found them a pleasure to have around, believing that when they grew up they would work and provide pretty things for her once again.

Patty

In 1935, Mila gave birth to another child, Patty. Things were not the same as they used to be. There were no more beautiful dresses, housekeepers, or even Warren to come home in the evening to help out. Warren was out of state searching for work and had no time or money to pamper Mila. She now had to live in a little grungy cabin, cook, wash, and clean for the family. Mila had no one to help her—and this kid had to be a girl.

Patty was always hungry and into things, with wet pants all the time. She was a lot of trouble. Mila didn't like it a bit. She had not raised the other kids, and now she was expected to raise this kid with practically nothing. She liked to go dancing and have fun, but this was not fun.

The Stoups had a daughter named Florence. She was married but seemed to have trouble keeping her husband's affections at home. She had a son who was four years old at the time. She asked her mother what she should do about getting her husband to stay at home. Her mother suggested she have another baby. That, however, was out of the question because Florence wanted to return to teaching.

Edith told Florence that the Hodge home, where they had gotten Betty and Ruby, had a baby and maybe she could get that baby girl. So Edith and Florence went to the Hodge home to see if the parents would give them the baby girl, who was a few months old.

Mila was on the porch washing clothes. Sitting in a tub of filthy black water was a baby about eight months old. Florence Varnum asked Mila if they could have the baby girl. They promised to take good care of her. Mila was delighted and said, "Sure, but I don't want her back, and I don't have any clothes for her. I'm glad to see her go, she's a lot of trouble."

"What is the baby's name?" Florence asked.

Mila answered, "Priscilla Gertrude." Bill and Richard had named her after their teachers. Now isn't that some name?

Edith and Florence took the baby, and on the way home they had to stop to buy diapers and clothing. When they arrived home, Betty had a picnic table set and food ready to eat. She was very surprised to see the baby climb up on the picnic table and eat several green olives. They all realized that this child had already learned how to find food when she was hungry.

They named her Patty Varnum—not legally, because they were not sure their scheme would work to keep Frances at home. If it didn't work, they would just find Patty another home. They had a birth certificate, but never used it for Patty's identification. How could they when Patty was using their name? The Varnums and the Stoups did lots of things that were illegal and just made up their own rules as they went along.

That was the summer of 1936. Shortly after getting Patty, the Varnums moved to Harlansburg, Pennsylvania. and needed help with Patty and other chores. Betty went to help out during the move, which delighted her because it meant she could spend time with her little sister.

The Rat

Betty was twelve years old at the time and loved playing with Patty. She would carry the baby around and run to see what Patty wanted at the first sign of a whimper. Florence told Betty, "I want you to stop spoiling Patty because you will soon be going back to the Stoups and leaving me with a spoiled brat."

Florence then took Patty upstairs for a nap. Soon, Patty began screaming horribly. Betty knew by the sound of the scream that something terrible was happening. Patty was not crying for attention. Betty snuck upstairs and peeked into the bedroom. There was blood everywhere. A huge rat was chewing on Patty's arm. Betty screamed for help, and Florence came running to see what had happened. Patty was taken to a hospital, treated, and given a tetanus shot—and Betty was sent back immediately to the Stoups for disobeying.

Patty got sick quite often with tonsillitis, ear infections, and childhood diseases—and once with scarlet fever. Florence was teaching in a little country school and couldn't take time off to care for her. When Patty got sick, she was taken to the Stoup farm to be cared for by her sisters. Somehow, Patty knew Betty and Ruby were her sisters, but she never asked questions, and her sisters were told never to tell her about their biological family. Patty spent most summers on the farm under the care of Betty and Ruby.

Little Baby Chicks

When Edith and Florence wanted to go shopping for the day, they would leave the three children in Betty's care on the farm. In addition to Ruby and Patty, there was Florence's son, Ronald. Betty was expected to do her daily chores, watch the children, and have dinner ready at five, when the women were expected to return from shopping.

Ruby and Ronald were close to the same age and could entertain themselves. It was Patty that Betty was concerned about because Patty was the quiet one, and Betty did not want to lose track of where she was. Betty turned on the radio and found some loud marching music. She gave Patty an old pot and a wooden spoon and showed her how to march and beat the drum. She also gave Patty two large aluminum lids to bang together to the tune of the marching music. When Patty was making noise, Betty could go out to feed the chickens, gather eggs, and do other outdoor chores. She knew where Patty was the entire time.

One day while Edith was away, a truck arrived to deliver large flat boxes of baby chicks. While Betty was outdoors doing chores, Patty decided to check on the baby chicks. There was chicken guano all over them, and they wouldn't stop peeping. Patty decided she would give them a bath so Betty wouldn't have to. She got a bucket of water (cold of course) and washed every baby chick in the boxes. She washed as much chicken guano out of the boxes as she could. All the baby chicks must have gone to sleep because they all stopped peeping. She was very proud of how she had helped Betty.

When Betty came in from her chores, Patty ran to tell her how helpful she had been. When Betty lifted the lid to the boxes, she saw that every baby chick was dead. When the Stoups arrived home that evening and found all the baby chicks dead, they were furious at Betty for permitting Patty to wash the chicks. Betty had to pay to replace all the chicks that died that day.

From then on, Betty took Patty along with her whenever she did chores outdoors.

Mr. Bear

Toys and dolls were not plentiful, and a lot of Patty's toys were made of clothespins and a piece of rag. Patty played in a sandbox using buds and full blooms of hollyhocks she placed together with toothpicks to create a line of dancing dolls of many colors that entertained her for hours.

When she went to the farm, she discovered a teddy bear she called Mr. Bear. She loved Mr. Bear and carried him around everywhere. When she went home to the Varnums, Mr. Bear stayed at the farm under Ruby's care.

The day Patty turned five years old, the mailman brought her a package. Excitedly, she opened it. There was Mr. Bear. He had clean fur and a new ribbon around his neck. Patty was so thrilled with her gift from Ruby. That night, she slept with Mr. Bear, but the next morning was a nightmare. Florence was yelling and whipping Patty because she had supposedly eaten crackers or something in bed the night before. Patty tried to tell her she hadn't eaten anything in bed.

Later, Edith told Florence that she had shown Ruby how to clean the bear's fur by rubbing salt and cornmeal onto the bear. Some had come out from inside the bear while Patty slept. Florence never ever said "I'm sorry."

The Beautiful Doll

After Betty graduated from high school, she got a job. She was determined to give her little sister Patty a beautiful doll for Christmas. She bought a doll with a beautiful dress, wool hair, and shoes. When Betty gave Patty the doll, Florence said, "Oh, she is too young for that doll. She does not know how to take care of such a beautiful doll, so I will put it away until she is older and then give it to her."

Months or years later, while cleaning a closet, Florence opened the box with the doll. Moths had eaten large holes in the dress and body, and all the wool on its head. Even its eyelashes were gone. There was nothing left but an ugly sight. The doll was thrown in the trash.

About thirty years later, Patty had a reoccurring dream where she was standing on a chair looking in an empty closet for something, but she didn't know what she was looking for. The closet was Betty's closet on the farm. Patty asked Betty if she knew why she was having this reoccurring dream. Betty told Patty about the doll she had given her. In her subconscious mind, Patty was still searching for her doll.

The Cow

Patty and Ruby were not just sisters but best friends as well, and they always got along very well. One Sunday, when Ruby was seven and Patty was three, they sat on the porch steps while Ruby read the comics out loud to Patty.

Edith told Ruby to go watch the cow so it wouldn't wonder off while grazing in an open field. Ruby took Patty and the comics and sat on a log by the field and read. They were so engrossed in the comics that they forgot all about the cow.

Suddenly, the phone rang. It was the neighbors informing Edith that her cow was in their garden devouring everything in sight. Ruby was beaten with a switch all the way down to the neighbors' to get the cow and all the way back home, crying so hard from the embarrassment and the pain. Patty cried too to see her sister whipped.

Ruby asked Patty, "Why are you crying? I'm the one who got the beating."

Patty hugged Ruby. It made her feel so sad to see her sister hurt when she felt she was to blame for Ruby getting in trouble.

Blackberry Bear

At an early age, Ruby learned how to bake the most delicious pies. Whatever fruit was in season, she would pick and make as many pies as she could in one day. The crust was always tender and flaky from the lard she used.

One summer day, when Patty was seven and Ruby was eleven, they decided to pick blackberries and make pies to sell in town. Ruby was allowed to keep the money she got from the pies so she could buy school clothes for the following year. They put on coveralls and long-sleeved shirts, got two large milk buckets from the barn, and started down the lane toward the berry patch.

They were singing, skipping, and laughing. Suddenly, they heard a loud roar. They stopped and looked up. There on the hill among the blackberry bushes stood a huge black bear on his hind legs, his arms open wide and his teeth showing.

The girls screamed, dropped their buckets, and ran to the house as fast as they had ever gone.

Edith asked, "What in the world is wrong with you girls?"

"We saw a huge black bear in the berry patch, and he stood up and roared at us," Ruby answered in a crying voice.

"We thought the bear was going to eat us or maybe tear us apart!" cried Patty.

"Nonsense," said Edith, "there are no bears in those woods. You girls would say anything to get out of doing work."

"Honest," Ruby replied, "there really was a bear in the berry patch by the woods."

The girls were ordered not to tell anyone this awful lie.

The following day was Sunday, and they wanted to tell their friends about their experience with the bear. They knew they must obey and not utter a word to anyone. When they returned home from church, the Sunday paper was on the porch. There, in bold letters, the headlines read: "Circus Wagon Overturns—Bear Escapes."

Both girl laughed and said, "See, we told you so!"

Back at Home

In 1939, Peter David was born to Mila and Warren Hodge. Something serious apparently happened to little David, who the family called Petie. He was very timid and serious, always polite and never sassy. He had the personality of his father, who had been very quiet and reserved. You could tell he had something on his mind, but he kept his thoughts to himself. For whatever the reason, David was never placed in foster care. He spent all his growing-up years in the Williard Home.

David Peter Hodge

Age 14   Age 16

Age 18

David's younger brother was named Joseph Bernard, but everyone called him Bernie. He was an adorable child and oh, how handsome he was as a teenager. When he was two or three years old, he was placed with foster parents who had no children of their own. They seemed to really love Bernie. His foster parents wanted badly to adopt him, but Warren Hodge would not permit it. Mr. Hodge always thought one day he would be financially able to gather his children and bring them home, but that day never came.

Bernie's foster parents gave him every material thing a boy could want. He had his own room with piles of games and toys, a new bike, and a pony. He was taught to take care of his things. Everything had a place, and he was to keep his room neat and his toys in order.

Everything was great until his foster mother had her own baby boy. Then, everything changed. The baby was the center of attention, and Bernie barely got any.

When the baby crawled and got into Bernie's things and tore them up while he was at school, Bernie was expected to clean up the mess. He didn't like it. He didn't like that kid and wished the kid had never been born.

One day Bernie thought he had purposely set the house on fire, but only the kitchen curtains ware burned. That was the last straw. Without any counseling or explanation, Bernie was taken back to the Williard Home with only the clothes on his back, a baseball and glove, and no return address. The foster parents never saw or contacted Bernie again. Bernie was heartbroken to be sent away, and yet he was glad to be away from that kid.

Joseph Bernard Hodge

Age 10

Age 12

Age 14

Oh, Brother, Another Girl

Mila Hodge gave birth to a baby girl in 1943. The child was placed in foster care three days after her birth with a very loving couple. This couple gave lots of kids foster care, but this little girl was special. They so wanted to adopt her, but again her biological father would not permit it. The foster dad died when the girl was five.

The foster mom promised to love and keep the girl even though the daddy had died, and declared that she would adopt her as soon as the law permitted. That time didn't come until the girl was twenty-one, but the foster mother did adopt her then, and she lived in that home until she was married. That is the reason she is not named.

Chapter 7

Having another child does not promise fidelity in any home. Bringing Patty to the Varnums did not accomplish what Florence had hoped for, so why have her hanging around like extra luggage? She really enjoyed being with her sisters. So the Varnums took Patty to live with her sister Betty, who was married by that time, in the summer of 1943. Patty was then seven years old. It was difficult financially for Betty. It was during World War II, and her husband, Donald, was away in the service. With Betty's baby girl, Karen, under a year old and so many things rationed, it was very hard to make ends meet on a soldier's pay.

There was a problem about sending Patty to school. Betty lived in Greenville, Pennsylvania, and most everybody knew she did not have a seven-year-old daughter. What would she tell the school so she would not have to pay tuition for Patty? After some thought, she decided to tell them that she and Patty were sisters, their parents had recently died in a car accident, and Patty had been left to her care.

The school accepted the story, and Patty was enrolled in second grade. One day, the teacher took Patty aside and explained that the students in her class were about to learn about the family tree. The teacher, having been told that Patty's parents had recently died, was concerned that what the class was about to learn might upset Patty. Betty had not told Patty what she had told the school, and upon hearing that her parents were dead, Patty became hysterical, screaming and crying, "No, no, my parents are not dead!"

The school had to call Betty to come and get her. No matter how Betty tried to console Patty and convince her that it was only a story she told the school, Patty believed what the teacher told her. She had screaming nightmares every night. Even after phone calls to the Varnums, nothing would change her mind until she could go home again with them. The Varnums did take Patty back to their home once again in Harlansburg.

Ruby

Meanwhile, Ruby was still living on the farm with the Stoups. With Edith quite ill at times, it became Ruby's responsibility to take care of most everything on the farm—including Howard Stoup's sexual needs. He started with Ruby when she was very young, telling her he would send her away if she told. Then he threatened to kill himself by driving his truck over the side of a bridge. It was threat after threat—but also gifts he bought to make her happy.

This had to be kept a secret because Howard Stoup was looked upon as a pillar in the community, an elder in the church, and a well-known carpenter who helped build many churches throughout the state. Ruby soon knew that this was all part of having a place to live—"doing her part." He was good to her otherwise and did not hurt her or beat her, so she just became accustomed to it.

Edith had a stroke and was partially paralyzed. She went to live with Florence. Within a few months, Howard got very ill, and Florence took him in too, which left Ruby without a home. She wanted to finish the high school she had been attending in Sandy Lake, Pennsylvania. She went to the Stoups' family physician and friend and offered to work for him in exchange for letting her live with his family until she graduated from high school.

Apparently, as men often do, Howard Stoup had told others his sex secrets. The doctor meant what he said when he told her she must pay him for staying there just as she had those previous years at the Stoups. He too took advantage of this young girl and sexually abused her, just as Mr. Stoup had done.

The doctor's wife discovered her husband's infidelity and threw Ruby out of her home. Ruby then went to live with Betty and her family, where she discovered she was pregnant. She took a bus to Sandy Lake and went to this same doctor. She was crying and so upset she could barely tell him that she was pregnant, but she did finally manage to ask what she should do. He explained that he would handle everything, and for her to just relax. He gave her a shot, and when she woke, she discovered she had had an abortion.

She cried again, saying, "I didn't come here for this. What have you done to me?"

He told her she would be just fine in a few days. He drove her to the foot of the steep hill near her sister's home. As she walked in the door, she fainted. Betty ran to her and, seeing she was hemorrhaging, tried to help her. She realized her sister had just had an abortion.

Betty was angry at both Ruby and this doctor for doing this awful thing; she didn't know until later that Ruby had only gone for advice, not an abortion. What these two men did to Ruby was rob her of good health, happiness, and her ability to have healthy children. Ruby was never well after that.

Howard Stoup died at the Varnum home in 1947. On his deathbed, he confessed that he had taken advantage of Ruby and had sexually abused her for many years, for his own needs, and begged for forgiveness. This was a shock to the family, but instead of taking the story as the truth, they blamed Ruby for it all. They shamed her, scorned her, and called her terrible names.

Both Ruby and Betty were banished from all Stoup family homes. The family tried to keep the girls from attending Howard's funeral that was held in the Stoups' home church in Sandy Lake. They were unsuccessful because the people of the church and the pastor knew both girls from when they had attended church with the Stoups for many years. Within days of the funeral, the Varnums tried to rid their home of Patty too.

Howard Stoup had included Betty, Ruby, and Patty in his will. If the girls could not be found, the confession from Howard could be forgotten, and they could also forget about giving those girls the money Howard had left them. How that will was broken is still unknown, but the three girls never got a cent or any household item that was promised to Betty or Ruby.

The Rock

It was Easter Sunday, 1947. The Varnums, Ronald, and Patty went to church in New Castle, Pennsylvania. After church, they went to a restaurant for lunch, and afterward they went for a ride. They went to a town that was not familiar to Patty. She asked, "What's the name of this town? Are we going to visit someone here?"

This is the rock that sits on the campus of Indiana State University in Indiana, Pennsylvania. Patty was told to sit on the rock and wait while Florence and Frances Varnum went to attempt to put Patty into the Williard Home because they did not want her as part of their family any longer.

Florence answered, "We have to go see a man about some business, I want you and Ronald to get out, sit on that rock, and wait for us. We will be back in a little while."

The rock sat on the campus of the Indiana State Teachers College in Indiana, Pennsylvania (now Indiana State University). Patty did as she was told—but Ronald, being restless and hearing music, said, "Come on, Pat, we're going to look this campus over." He headed straight for the music hall. Patty said, "We'd better not, Ron. If they come back and we aren't at the rock, we'll be in big trouble."

"Nah," Ronald said. "I'll tell them it was my idea."

Inside the music hall, Ron found a piano and played several songs. He sure could play the piano! The two strolled around the campus for about a half hour, and then Ronald and Patty returned to the rock to wait. Within a few minutes, the Varnums returned, and no more was said about the trip to Indiana.

Candy Kisses

Two months later, Florence and Francis Varnum took Patty for a long ride in the car. They had something to tell her, and they didn't need for her to make a scene for the neighbors to hear. It was a ride she would never forget. They took along a bag of candy kisses, perhaps to help "sweeten" the blow.

They told her that her name was not Patty Varnum. It was Priscilla Gertrude Hodge. Patty said, "I don't like that name, and I want to keep my old name." She saw no reason to change it.

The Varnums saw a reason, and the reason was that she was not their child and could no longer live with them or carry their name. They said, "You told lies and made up stories, and we just cannot put up with you any longer."

Patty asked, "Where am I going to live?"

Florence answered, "You have a sister that lives in New Castle, and we are going to take you to her and let you live with her."

Patty asked, "Could I come back home later?"

Florence answered, "*No.* We took care of you for several years. We have plans now, and you will have to stay somewhere else, not with us."

They had packed her clothes in a box, and they drove to Patty's sister Bertha's apartment in New Castle, Pennsylvania. The Varnums told Patty to sit on the stairs leading to the apartment and wait until Bertha and her husband, Bob, returned from work. Then they drove away.

Patty was twelve and emotionally distraught, heartbroken, and angry. She felt lost and helpless. She was sick at her stomach and felt like throwing up. What if this sister who she did not know didn't want her either? What would happen to her? Where would she go?

Life with Bertha

Bertha came home from work and found Patty sitting on the steps with a box of clothes beside her. She knew by the look on Patty's face that she didn't just come for a visit but that Patty had been dumped in her lap. They had never lived together at home or anywhere, and now living in a small one-bedroom apartment, with Bertha newly married, made things quite uncomfortable. Patty was very unhappy living with Bob and Bertha. She felt a strong tension between her and her sister.

It wasn't like the relationship she had with her other two sisters. She knew them and loved them, and they loved her. But since the Varnums had disowned Betty and Ruby, Florence could not ask either of them to take Patty. Bertha was the only resource left. Florence really didn't care if the relationship worked or not, as long as she was rid of Patty.

Patty slept on a rollaway bed in the living room. She had no privacy, and neither did Bob and Bertha. She felt bad that she was in the way and not wanted, but she had nowhere else to go.

Patty woke every morning to the smell of coffee perking. The smell sickened her, and she began dry heaving. She was only twelve, and having had the stability rug pulled out from under her, she was living in limbo.

Patty had just lost her childhood home, and the people she had believed were her parents had deserted her. Living now with people she did not know, knowing she was not welcome there, and knowing she was in the way made her sick and scared to death. Apparently, Bertha did not see or understand Patty's emotional condition. She could only see that this girl had disrupted her home and her marriage. This made Bertha angry, and she didn't know what to do about it.

Patty had five sisters. Four are pictured here with Patty at her son's graduation party. Patty has just met Dorothy a few days prior to the party. Dorothy has never been seen or heard from since. The other sisters have all since passed. Patty's fifth sister was adopted as an adult and has nothing to do with her biological family.

Betty, Bertha, Dorothy, Ruby, Patty

Patty had dry heaves nearly every morning, so Bertha just knew Patty had to be pregnant—that was the reason for the Varnums getting rid of her. Bertha called the Varnums and accused them of that, which they denied. She insisted that they prove it by taking Patty to a doctor for an examination. They did, and at age twelve, Patty had her first exam.

The doctor assured the Varnums that Patty was not pregnant. On the way back to the apartment, Patty begged them, "Please let me go home with you. I promise I'll be very good." They said no and once again dropped Patty off outside her sister's apartment. When Patty opened the door to the apartment, Bertha was waiting angrily, thinking that Patty was pregnant and the Varnums had gone away leaving this pregnant girl for her to tend to. Patty tried to tell her that the doctor said she was not pregnant, but Bertha did not believe her.

Bertha took Patty back to the doctor and demanded he do another exam with her present. The doctor was furious and told her he would not do it again, that she had to take his word for it that this girl was definitely not pregnant. Bertha said she didn't believe him and that she would take Patty to another doctor.

The doctor said angrily, "What are you people doing to this girl? If you take her to another doctor I will press charges against you. Do you understand me?"

Bertha answered, "Yes." There was no further discussion about that subject.

The Belt

Bertha's anger became worse. For anything at all, she would beat Patty with a belt. When she got tired, Bob would beat the girl. Patty tried to take cover by crawling under the bed or hiding in a closet behind clothes. That made them even angrier, and the belt always found her. This continued until a neighbor in an upstairs apartment turned them in for abuse.

Patty had only lived with them for four months and had changed schools three times. Now it was time for Patty to find another home. Her sister had had enough. Bertha packed a box with Patty's clothes and drove her to Alverta, Pennsylvania. There, on a little hill, stood a hunting shack where the girls' parents lived. It had two small rooms and no furnace but was heated with two wood-burning stoves—one in the kitchen for cooking and a small stove in the bedroom that doubled as a living room. There was no running water, just a pump in the yard. There was no indoor bathroom, just an outhouse in the backyard.

Bertha asked her dad if he would take Patty because she didn't know what else to do with her. He answered, "I will, if Patty wants to stay." He asked Patty and she said yes. Patty was in seventh grade and was now attending her fourth school that year.

Patty's dad, Warren Hodge, tried to make it comfortable for her and tried to provide anything she wanted or needed. But Mila did not welcome her daughter home. Suddenly she had another mouth to feed—and wash and iron for. They even had to share a bed. Mila was also terribly jealous of the attention Warren gave this intruder.

Warren saw how unhappy his daughter was and knew that he was not providing the proper environment for her. He called child welfare and asked to have a social worker come and take Patty to the Williard Home or place her in foster care.

Back to the Rock

Mrs. Long was the director of the department of child welfare. She had a long black Chrysler. As Mrs. Long drove along, Patty looked out the window. Suddenly, she realized she had been here before. She saw Indiana State College with the rock on campus but still did not know where the Varnums had gone that day or why.

Mrs. Long told Patty that she had a brother named Pete in the Williard Home, and a brother and sister in foster care. Patty didn't say anything;

she just wondered why these people who called themselves her parents had so many children they didn't want and certainly couldn't afford. Since she had been taught long ago not to ask questions, she kept her thoughts to herself.

The matron, Mrs. Rowley, was sick and in the hospital when Patty arrived at the Williard Home. No adult was there to greet her, but Johnny Mari came around the corner and offered to carry her bags in. Mrs. Long thanked him for being so nice.

Patty sat on the end of the radiator bench, stared out the window, and cried. She was lonely and scared. It was an awful feeling to know that you had no one who loved or cared about you and you had no home. Johnny came to the outside of the window and said, "Don't cry, it's not too bad here. You'll get used to it, you'll see. I'll be your friend, okay?"

The boys and girls were separated most of the time. The boys were to be outside or in the basement playroom, and the girls were to stay in the upstairs playroom and entertain the younger children.

It was shortly after being put in the Williard Home that Patty realized where the Varnums went the day she was told to sit on the rock and wait for their return. They had gone there to leave her at the Williard Home. They were told that the Williard Home was a county home and they had to have residence in Indiana County. They could not just drop a child off like an animal at an animal shelter. A social worker had to visit the home and determine if this was the best move for the child.

Since the Varnums did not live in Indiana County, they knew that they had to find somewhere else to send this girl. That's why they took her to her sister Bertha's without even telling or asking her sister. What would they do if her sister said no?

Chapter 8

In the summer of 1949, Mrs. Gray, Patty's assigned social worker, announced that she had found a very nice foster home for her. Patty asked, "Please, can I stay in the Williard Home?"

Mrs. Gray said, "No, Patty, we have to place you in foster care. There are so many other children that are in unhealthy homes and need to go to the Williard Home for a while. We must make room for them."

So Patty spent the summer of 1949 on a milk farm. It was work from early morning until late at night. It was Patty's responsibility to wash the many milk machines, candle eggs, bathe the three young children, clean, cook, bake, hang clothes, and paint. Her foster parents accepted the pay the county sent plus expected more and more work from their little chore girl.

Patty was in need of shoes, so child welfare sent a requisition for the purchase of one pair of shoes. This requisition was a large yellow piece of paper about eight by twelve inches. It was so embarrassing to have the salesperson open the paper and read it. Patty just knew everyone in the shoe store realized she was from the orphanage getting a pair of shoes from child welfare.

That foster home didn't work out. Patty was not happy. All she could think about was losing her home with the Varnums. If only she had been good, maybe they wouldn't have sent her away. Child welfare was asked to come and get this girl. Mrs. Gray went to the work farm, removed Patty, and took her back to the Williard Home, where she stayed for another winter.

The following summer, child welfare tried again. This time, Patty was placed in the same foster home that her younger sister was living in. This way the two sisters might bond, and it would bring happiness to both girls,

But that did not happen. The little sister was not thrilled to have to share her home with this big girl who was called her sister. She was robbed of her privacy. She had to share her bed and her room and "her family." Patty also served as a reminder that she had a biological family. She was very content with being a part of *this* family. Why did Patty have to come along and spoil it for her?

Patty did not know why her little sister didn't like her, but years later she understood perfectly that her sister's feelings were much like her own. Her sister had been placed in that home when she was three days old. This was the only family she'd ever known, and suddenly a teenage girl she'd never seen before who called herself her sister was in her home, in her room, in her bed, taking attention that was rightfully hers. It was an uncomfortable situation, just like it was for Patty when she was taken to live with Bertha, a sister she did not know.

Also in the home was a son named Walter. One Saturday, the mother told Walter, who was sixteen, and Patty, who was fifteen, to go downstairs and clean the cellar. When the two got down to the cellar, instead of working, Walter became very sexually aggressive. Patty ran upstairs crying. Walter's sister, Eleanor, asked, "Patty, why are you crying?"

Patty told Eleanor. Eleanor said, "Go tell Mom what Walter did."

Patty went upstairs where their mother was resting and told her what happened. She replied, "I will question my son and get back with you, Patty." Later that day she did talk to Patty and said, "My son denied your allegations, and I believe my son!"

Patty said okay—but the following school day, instead of returning to her foster home, Patty went to child welfare. She told Mrs. Gray what had happened and said, "I don't want to live there any longer." She gave her reasons why.

To Patty's surprise, Mrs. Gray agreed, and Patty was quickly removed from that home. Several months after Patty had gone back to the Williard Home, she was walking home by herself after a school activity. Walter pulled up beside her with his car and offered her a ride home. Patty refused the ride. Walter apologized for his previous behavior and drove away.

Linda and Janet

Teenagers from the Williard Home were bused to the Indiana Joint High School. Patty joined several clubs there: mixed chorus, nurses club, home nursing, and ushers club. She loved being involved and was very active in each club.

Patty also worked for several people in town. She babysat, cleaned house, and ironed, but her favorite job was working for Tony Recoopereo. He owned Rustic Lodge, an Italian restaurant about a quarter mile from the Williard Home. Patty helped serve large picnics on the huge shady grounds of the restaurant. Sometimes she washed dishes or cleaned the secret card room upstairs that only a few people knew about. Once she cleaned cupboards for Tony's wife at their home. Patty also did ironing for Mrs. Merrill, the Williard Home matron. Patty loved children and often chose to read to or entertain young children rather than do housework.

When Patty was seventeen, there was a family in crises. Both husband and wife were alcoholics. They would leave their children alone at night while they drank at the bar. Not having fed her daughters any dinner, the mother would bring home a candy bar and toss it in the bed with the girls, who were two and four years old. They also had a son about six years old who they usually took to the bar with them. The boy became very ill, and the parents took him to the emergency room.

The boy had pneumonia and had to be hospitalized. The parents did not have insurance or money to pay for their son's care. The case was turned over to a social worker. Within a few days, the social worker visited the home and asked to see the other children. The mother stated that they were both sleeping and told the social worker to come back another time.

The social worker left but returned the following day and again requested to see the children. The mother claimed there was no light in their room and they were sleeping. This time, the social worker insisted on seeing the girls and said she would light a match, which she did. When she looked into the crib, she was horrified to find them in such condition. The two little girls were barely conscious, and their bellies were swollen big and round, a sign of starvation.

She left the home and called the police and an ambulance. The mother was arrested for child neglect, and the girls were immediately hospitalized. They were in intensive care for over a month and in special care for two more months. They were then taken to the Williard Home but kept in isolation for several weeks. Finally they were strong enough to be put with the other children. Patty was put in charge of caring for Linda, the two-year-old, who could not walk, talk, or eat solid food and was still wearing diapers.

Janet

Linda

Patty & Linda

Patty

It was summer, and Patty was out of school, so she devoted most of her time to working and to playing and teaching Linda. By the end of summer, Linda was beginning to say words, walk, play, laugh, and eat solid foods. Still, her stomach protruded.

The parents went on trial. Their two girls and their little boy did not remember the abuse and neglect they had suffered. As they entered the courtroom there was a happy reunion between the parents and their children. It appeared to the jury that the children had not suffered too much because they looked so healthy and happy. The children were given back to their parents.

This was devastating to Patty—so much so that she became very ill and was in isolation for close to a month. She was a senior in high school and feared having missed so much school that she would not graduate. But Patty had been a good student, and she did graduate that June of 1954. As soon as Patty graduated, she was on her own. She rented a room and got a job working in a restaurant in town.

This is the Indiana High School graduation picture of
Patty Hodge in 1954. She was eighteen years old.

One day she went back to the Williard Home to visit. Mrs. Merrill
said, "Look who's back." It was Linda and Janet and their brother. Their
mother had struck Linda with a stick and had put the girl's eye out. This
was a terrible blow to Patty because she had truly loved that child. To
know that Linda's mother had abused her again just made Patty sick,

The parents never got their children back, and Patty said, "Too bad, and Linda never got her vision back either."

A Very Pretty Ring

In December 1954, Johnny asked Patty to marry him. Of course she said yes, and for her nineteenth birthday, Johnny gave Patty an engagement ring. They set their wedding date for the following August. In the meantime, Patty continued working at the restaurant, and Johnny went back to Michigan to work at the Edison Company. They really wanted to be together but knew they must wait until they were married and Johnny could afford a place for them to live.

Johnny and Patty were invited to spend Christmas with Johnny's sister Julia and her family in Pittsburgh. When Johnny went to get Patty to go to his sister's, he got a surprise: Patty was all packed ready to move to Michigan. Patty got a surprise too because Johnny's brother Ed was with him.

It turned out to be a good thing because Johnny asked Ed if Patty could stay with Emma and him until they could get her a room. Ed said, "Sure she can."

Patty moved to Dearborn and got a job at Bell Telephone. She later got a job at Abstract and Title Company, working as a file clerk and elevator operator, and she was soon promoted to the recording department. She recorded mortgage titles written by hand into huge books that weighed twenty pounds each.

Just before Johnny and Patty were married on August 22, 1955, Johnny bought a brand-new beautiful thirty-foot mobile home. Patty quit working for Abstract and Title Company because of the distance traveling to work. It meant transferring buses twice, which made it difficult getting to work on time. She went to work for Scott Paper, making tissues and table napkins. She worked there for two years, until she was four months pregnant.

Part III

Chapter 9

Johnny and Patty's son Thomas was born on June 27, 1958. Within days of the baby's birth, they were looking for a house. The mobile home was just too small. Tommy's crib sat on top of the bathtub, and there was very little closet space. They had baby clothes stacked on top of theirs.

They moved into their brand-new home on Wohlfiel Street in Taylor, Michigan, in June of 1959. That same month, Tommy turned one year old. They had very little money and no furniture when they moved, so they bought furniture from an old woman who was selling hers.

Tommy was born on
June 27, 1958

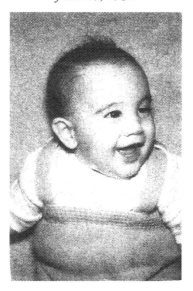

Tommy Mari, six months old

There were waxed hardwood floors throughout the house, but since they had not been varnished, they were very hard to keep up. Wall-to-wall carpeting was in style at the time, so eventually the floors were carpeted.

Johnny and Patty were determined to have a small family, to work hard, to keep their bills paid, and to not to have a lot of debt. As an employee of the Detroit Edison Company, Johnny was able to purchase all their appliances through the company without any interest, which helped a lot. The company deducted a dollar or two each week from his paycheck. Johnny worked hard over the years and worked every bit of overtime that was offered to him. He began working evenings with an electrician friend, Allen Clark, wiring new churches in the community. Johnny came home so tired at night, but he was up bright and early each morning.

He and Patty enjoyed doing things together as a family—simple things like picnics, going to the beach, or visiting family in Pennsylvania. Another thing they loved doing was taking a carload of teenagers to the Masonic Temple in Detroit once a month for Youth for Christ meetings. Johnny also worked with a group of boys eight to ten years of age from the church. It was called Boy's Brigade.

Sometimes after church Johnny would round the boys up and ask if they wanted to go to the beach, swim, toss a ball, and eat hot dogs, chips, and a soda. The boys always enjoyed spending time with Johnny, and Johnny enjoyed the time he spent with them. He always found time to talk to each boy separately. Sometimes it was spiritual, and other times the boy just needed someone to share a problem with or tell something special that was happening in his life.

A New Addition

Susan was born on August 2, 1963. She was a very special child, or at least Johnny and Patty felt she was—quiet, obedient, and tender-hearted. As a young child, she often had high fevers, tonsillitis, and ear and upper-respiratory infections. Patty took Susie to the doctor at least nine times one year. Penicillin was the drug of the day, and every time she went to the doctor, Susie was given a penicillin shot and liquid penicillin to take for a week.

Before Susie started school, they recognized that there was a problem with her speech. Patty spent a lot of time with Susie slowly breaking down words into syllables and sounds. When Susie started school, her speech was improved but not real clear.

Their son Tommy was in the fourth grade and attending a Christian school. Johnny and Patty were just sure that Christian school was also the place for Susie. Surely the loving kind teachers would want to spend time helping her with her speech, but that did not happen. Susie was in kindergarten and her teacher's name was Mrs. Richie. Susie pronounced it "Mrs. Witchie." All the children laughed and the teacher was embarrassed.

Mrs. Richie called Patty, telling her that she felt it would be best if they took Susan out of school and waited another year for her to gain maturity, as she was not paying attention or answering when spoken to. If they would not take her out of school, then Susan must go to a different class because she would not tolerate Susan calling her "Mrs. Witchie."

The school principal thought the teacher knew what was best for the child, and Susan was removed from the Christian school. Within a year, Tommy left the school also. He was bright and got good grades but was overactive, and it was difficult for him to sit quietly. Something was always moving—his feet, his hands, or his mouth. So the school informed his parents that Tommy would have to be put on Ritalin or leave the Christian school.

The family doctor was consulted to see if that was the best thing to do. He recommended taking Tommy out of Christian school and putting him into public school. He then suggested that Tommy walk to school and walk home for lunch. He was to have a quiet lunch including at least half a cup of coffee.

This was December. The Taylor School District had been on strike since September, but it was now back in session. Patty took Susan to the neighborhood elementary school, explained the situation to the principal, and asked for his opinion. He placed Susan in a class with a teacher with many years of experience. Mrs. Moss had been Tommy's kindergarten teacher. He remembers vividly how dedicated and loving she was to each child in the class—how she got down on her knees and helped them button or zip each of their coats or made sure their boots were on the right foot.

Mrs. Moss took Susan into her class and observed her for two weeks. Then she and the principal met with Patty and John so Mrs. Moss could share what she had observed. She began by commenting what a quiet, sweet girl Susan was. However, she felt that when Susan did not respond when spoken to or take part in games or conversations with other children, it was because she did not hear what was said. She particularly observed Susan while reading the children a story. Instead of showing an interest in the story as the other children were, Susan sat quietly looking around or looking to see what the other children were doing.

Mrs. Moss said that in her opinion, Susan should be tested for a hearing impairment. Tests were done, and they showed she did have an impairment, but she also had fluid behind the eardrum, which could cause a hearing impairment and could be improved by draining the ears. Her tonsils and adenoids were removed, and her ears were drained. Eight weeks later, another hearing test was preformed. It showed a permanent moderate hearing loss. Susan had to be fitted with one or two hearing aids.

Special Education

Because of her hearing loss, Susan was placed in a special-education class. This was 1968, seven years before it became law that every child had a right to an education. Local school districts had a few classes called "special education," but they weren't classes to help educate the many types of handicapped children who needed help. They were mostly for the benefit of the classroom teachers, so they would not have to spend class time with special-needs students. There was also no separation between the different handicapped children. They were all grouped together.

Susan was bused twenty miles and placed in a class of eight to eleven children who had many different special needs. Some students were mentally handicapped or autistic, blind, deaf, or hearing impaired. The poor teacher had no aide, and there was nothing but confusion. She was not able to teach anything to anyone, because each child had his or her individual problems to be dealt with. The teacher got one break and that was for lunch, when the principal sat in for her.

The principal could see this class was not working. The teacher badly needed an aide and the students needed to be put into separate classes, where each child could be given some individual help for his special needs. This was beyond the principal's jurisdiction.

Special education required a lot of funding that the school districts did not have. It required specially trained teachers for each special need and special equipment for the needs of the different learning disabilities. This program needed state and federal aid.

That year, parents of the students were asked to volunteer their help so the teacher could work one-on-one with the students. Patty volunteered four days out of five. It helped a lot, but there just weren't enough hours in the day for the teacher to help each student with his or her particular need. She was not trained in all those fields of special education, nor did she have equipment necessary for many of her students. Each student was on a different learning or grade level. Susan learned very little that school year.

As each year passed, her schooling improved, and for the next four years she was in a class of hearing-impaired and deaf students. This was very difficult for the teacher because they were not allowed to use sign language with the hearing-impaired students, but many of the deaf students' only language was sign.

On the bus, on the playground, or in the classroom, the hearing-impaired children were quickly picking up sign language, and they preferred to use it rather than speak. The following year, the deaf and hearing-impaired students were separated into different classes.

These were not fun years for Susan. She was just a little girl. She had to get up very early; eat breakfast, which was hard for her so early in the morning; be dressed warm in the winter with boots, hearing aide, and lunch packed; and be ready for the long bus ride to school. It was dark when she left and dark when she arrived home. Most evenings, she would be sound asleep by the time the bus dropped her off.

Susan was eight years old and in the third grade when she decided to take a small doll to school with her so she and a friend could play on the ride to school and home. She had taken the doll for about a week when her teacher called saying that she found this unusual and disturbing, and she had asked the school psychologist to meet with Patty to decide if this was damaging to Susan psychologically.

That was crazy talk to Patty, but she agreed to meet with the psychologist to see why they felt that a doll would hurt anyone psychologically. Patty was told that the teacher felt Susan was so attached to the doll that she could not go to school without it, but she also stated that upon entering the classroom, Susan took the doll and put it on the bookshelf as instructed and left it there until it was time to go home. The teacher and the psychologist felt the children might make fun of her for bringing a doll to school.

When Patty explained that it was a means of entertainment for her and another little girl as they rode the bus for two hours and really nothing more, he thought differently about it and stated that Susan should be allowed to take the doll to school but Patty should be aware that the children might make fun of her. Patty told Susan that perhaps she should leave her dolly at home because it might get broken. Susan accepted that and left the doll at home, but she fell asleep nearly every evening before she got home.

Family in Italy

About this time, Johnny began wondering about his father's family in Italy. He knew his father had come from Ischia di Castro, Italy, at age nineteen, but that was all he knew. Johnny wondered if he had any relatives still living. He went to his aunt Rose and asked her. She told him she did not know, but that she knew there was a woman living in Dearborn, Michigan, who knew Julius—they had come to America on the same ship. She gave Johnny a name, and he found the son of that woman. He went to visit the man and discovered the man's mother was living right there with her son and his family.

She didn't speak English, but her son interpreted for her. For a while, she could not remember having known Gulio Mari. But suddenly, she remembered. This family had a cousin who lived in a town near Ischia di Castro, worked in the municipal building, and could get much-needed information there as well as contact Johnny's extended family to see if he could visit. Within a week, Johnny had received a letter from his two aunts and their families stating that they were so excited about his visit.

This was 1968. Johnny was planning to travel to the Holy Land with a church group. This was exciting because he had always wanted to go to the Holy Land and visit the places our Lord had walked. Since the group was going to visit several places in Italy, he took the opportunity to visit his family during the tour of Rome. The man who located Johnny's family had a son, Anthony, who was studying to be a doctor and could read, write, and speak English fluently.

Anthony took Johnny to meet Aunt Anna and Aunt Madelina, who were quite elderly and ill. These ladies were so delighted to see Johnny. When Johnny walked into Madelina's room, she was praying. She looked up and saw Johnny and cried out, "Oh, Gulio, Gulio, you have come home."

Anthony went to Madelina and said, "This man is Johnny, Gulio's son. He has come to visit you."

Anthony interpreted for Johnny and his father's family and got them all acquainted. This was a short but exciting visit for Johnny and for his two aunts.

Aunt Anna was confined to her bed before Johnny's visit, but later she felt well enough to get up. The family so wanted to meet Johnny's brothers and sisters and insisted that Johnny bring all of them for a visit.

The following year, Johnny arranged to take his brothers and sisters to Italy so they too could meet their father's family. Ed, Rose Marie, Julia (along with her sixteen-year old-daughter, Cindy), Eileen (Tom's wife), and Johnny all flew to Italy that spring. It was a wonderful trip to be able to visit the aunts who had dearly loved and missed their brother Gulio. Most of the extended Mari family gathered at the aunts' house, and the reunion was wonderful.

Anthony was not able to be there, so communication was difficult. Somehow by the end of the week, they seemed to understand each other.

Time did not allow for further research on his mother while Johnny visited his father's family. His mother had come from a different area of Italy, and no one knew where to look. Johnny discovered his search for his mother's heritage was nearly impossible.

He asked relatives, wrote letters, and searched through ship records and church records to find who his mother's parents were, especially her mother. How did she get to America? Who brought her here? There were no ship records to show Raphaela (his grandmother) coming to America with a child. Johnny so hoped he would learn what he needed to know before he died.

The Fight

Life was rolling along pretty well for Johnny and Patty and their family. In high school, Susan was integrated into all regular classes with only a study hall with a special-education teacher to assist. One day, Susan and another girl got into a quarrel, and it ended up in a fight. The other girl grabbed Susan's hearing aid and threw it down the hall, where it hit the wall. The hearing aid broke. Both girls were sent to the office. The other girl told the principal that Susan had started the fight, and she was only defending herself.

Susan was mainly concerned about her hearing aid being broken. She tried to tell the principal that the other girl had pulled off her hearing aid and threw it, but the other girl denied doing that and said it had fallen off during the fight. Believing the other girl's story, the principal gave Susan three days' suspension while the other girl got nothing.

Susan arrived home very upset and crying over being suspended and even worse having had her hearing aid broken. Patty called the school to get details on this problem and asked why she had not been notified or why the special-education teacher had not been present at the meeting with the principal. Patty was told that the principal made the decision, and he felt no need to involve the special-education teacher. Patty asked if he was aware that the hearing aid had been broken during the fight. He said he was and suggested they turn a report in to their homeowner's insurance, since it would probably pay for a new aid.

For the next three days, Patty and Susan picketed the school with signs declaring the unfairness of the decision and asking for a meeting. The student council came out and asked questions, but Patty told them it was vitally important she speak to a school official. No official responded to her request.

The homeowner's insurance company was notified, and a young woman was sent out to the home to make a report. She listened as Susan told what happened. The investigator asked if Susan could give her names of those who had witnessed the fight or who had seen the girl throw the hearing aid. Susan named two teachers.

The investigator said she needed to interview people at the school for her report. She returned saying that no one seemed to know who started the fight, but the teachers knew that the hearing aid had been thrown. If it had fallen off, it would not have traveled several feet from the girls and hit a wall.

There was a witness who stated the other girl had thrown Susan's hearing aid down the hallway. This investigator spoke to the principal and reported what the witnesses—both teachers and students—stated had really happened.

That evening, the principal phoned Patty and apologized, saying he had spoken to the parents of the other girl and their insurance would pay for the hearing aid. Because the other girl was a swimming champ, she was not disciplined for her part in the fight or for breaking Susan's hearing aid. The rule was that if an athletic student was suspended for misbehavior, then he or she could not participate in any competition or games. Since this girl was a champion swimmer and a competition was coming up, the principal simply could not suspend her. She was too valuable to the team.

The investigator had a younger sister who was also hearing impaired and had experienced a similar incident. The investigator was aware of the unfair treatment special-education students often got because they were not able to express themselves.

Chapter 10

It was the summer of 1981 when Johnny was transferred to St. Clair, Michigan, to work as a substitute foreman at the St. Clair Power Plant. The foreman for that job was on sick leave. Warren Spalding was a good friend and coworker of Johnny's, and he offered to let Johnny park his small travel trailer on Warren's property while he worked at the St. Clair plant. This was ideal because it was close to work and yet private and quiet, so Johnny was able to rest better than if he stayed in a hotel. Johnny worked that job the entire summer, going home on weekends.

When the man returned to his job who had been sick, Johnny wondered where he would be sent to work. To his surprise, he was offered a permanent job as a supervisor at the Bell River Power Plant that was just beginning to be built. Since this job was permanent, the company offered to move his family and pay for his home so he could buy another home.

Johnny and his family moved to St. Clair, Michigan. Tom joined the Coast Guard, and Susan finished her last two years of high school. After Susan graduated, Johnny, Patty, and Susan moved to Port Huron. Patty had one year completed toward an associate's degree from Wayne County Community College. She completed her degree with a cum laude honor.

It was Patty's desire to open her own child-care center, but the community they had moved to didn't need one. Since Patty had worked for the Wayne County Intermediate School District a year or so earlier, she applied at the St. Clair Intermediate School District and was hired as a teacher's aide. The children she worked with ranged in age from three to twenty-six. They were severely mentally impaired as well as trainable, autistic, and physically impaired. She worked there for ten years and retired shortly after Johnny retired after thirty-seven years with the Detroit Edison Company.

A Wedding

Tom married Linda Garcia in May of 1988. It was a beautiful wedding and a really fun reception. Many relatives from both sides of the family were there. Tom worked in outside construction and Linda was a cashier for A&P and later for Farmer Jack's Supermarkets. Linda had worked for eight years and really wanted to work two more years and retire, but she stopped working for a while to have a baby. Nicole was born February 5, 1992.

Who better than Grandma Mari to take care of Nicole? But she and Grandpa Mari were living up in Port Huron. Since both were retired, Tom asked if they would consider moving closer to him and Linda to help care for Nicole. Patty and Johnny agreed and moved to Westland, Michigan, just a few blocks from their son. Susan bought an older but beautiful house trailer and she and Kilo, her leader dog, were very happy there.

Nicole was now walking and talking and wanting to play with other children, but she was still too young to go to preschool. She went to daycare in a lady's home and learned to play and share with other children.

Johnny and Patty's son, Tom,
was married to Linda Garcia in May 1988

Heartaches and Joys

Through the years, Johnny and Patty had talked about moving to Florida after retirement. The subject came up again—but suddenly, Johnny had a heart attack. They thought at first that their hopes and dreams of moving would never happen, but Johnny recovered nicely and knew that Florida's mild weather was conducive to good health. Johnny, Patty, and Susan moved to Spring Hill, Florida, in August of 1995.

While moving heavy furniture, Johnny pulled a double hernia. He had to have surgery to repair both hernias. One side developed a serious infection, which required removing the grid. The wound was healing on the outside first instead of the inside, so much cleansing and attention were given to the wound. Susan attended to her dad's surgery wounds like a pro. Patty was not home. She was in Michigan substituting so she could begin collecting retirement from the Michigan State Employees Retirement System and Social Security.

It took seven months for Johnny's wounds to heal. On August 7, 1997, Johnny suffered another heart attack, and this time he required a four-way bypass. He did well, however, and gained his strength back quickly. He was soon doing tasks and riding his bike.

On November 27, 1998, Susan got very ill with both viral and bacterial pneumonia. Her illness was misdiagnosed, and she was treated for sinusitis. She had a very high fever and very low blood pressure. She was hospitalized for four days and died on December 3, 1998.

This felt like the worst heartache and loss Johnny and Patty had ever experienced, and it just wouldn't stop. Life lost meaning for them after Susie's death. She had always lived so close to her parents and that was the reason she had moved to Florida with them. Now she was gone. The old hurt, the old pain of loss was back. Oh, how it hurt.

Nicole was a very precious child to Johnny and Patty, and she played a very important role in healing their lives. Not that anyone could take the place of Susan, but Nicole was very loving and spent a lot of time visiting her grandparents. She grew to be a beautiful young woman. After high school, Nicole took two years training through the EMS. She took college classes and worked several different jobs to find what she would like to do best in life.

She went to dental college and completed a dental assistant's course. She worked several months until she took a leave to have a baby. Her baby boy, named Jacob, was born March 24, 2015. Nicole plans to return to college to be certified as a hygienist.

Tom thought for many years that he had more than just a job. He considered it a career. He worked in water purification and filtration for twenty years. He had worked for Seamens Corporation for five years. He studied, went to classes and seminars, and kept up with the latest changes in industry and equipment. Whatever job he was on, he made sure it was done correctly, in proper order, and if possible on time.

He had worked his way up to the top of his pay scale. One day as he completed a job, he was told that management was laying him off. This nearly killed him, and later he realized a man he had trained had been given his job. The recession kept him from finding another job in the field of water. He tried to find full-time work without success. He did any kind of day work just to feed his family. Thank goodness his wife had a job working at the airport at TSA, which helped a lot.

When Linda's mother passed away, it broke Linda's heart, for they had been very close. Her father had been very ill for several years with diabetes. He also had a bad heart. Complications set in, and he died in 2011. She has three brothers, but she had been the one who took on the responsibility of caring for her dad's affairs. Just about this same time, Linda was diagnosed with breast cancer and had to undergo surgery, chemotherapy, and radiation.

This had been a terrible two years for Tom. No work, no income, his wife sick with cancer, and so many bills to pay. He worked any little side job he could find and put in hundreds of applications to get steady work. Finally, after two years, he saw an ad online for a job in a town near his home. He applied, had two interviews, and was hired. It was exactly what he had been trained to do, and he knew the work well. The company was very happy to find a man who could do all the different jobs that they needed.

At present, Johnny works with disabled veterans, recommending a good officer who will help veterans get physical and financial aid they so deserve. Patty helps out by printing hundreds of envelopes for these disabled veterans.

Even though Johnny and Patty had very hard and sad childhoods, they realized there was no benefit in living in the past. They were determined to make a happy marriage, to live debt-free if they could, to raise their children with high standards both spiritually and morally, and to trust Christ as their Savior and let Him guide and direct their lives and their children's lives.

A Mystery Solved

By 2012, Johnny had finally given up trying to find who his mother was. Then one day Johnny's sister-in-law called Tom—Johnny and Patty's son—over to her home. She said she had something to tell him. She had kept a secret for many, many years and had promised she would never tell. She knew that Johnny had searched for answers concerning his mother, so she decided to tell Tom the story. She said that while living in Italy, although Donald Cuozzo Sr. was married to Raphaela, he had an affair with a very young girl, and she became pregnant. Donald left Italy and came to America, where he lived in Fulton Run and worked as a coal miner. Raphaela knew where he lived.

The girl's parents went to the priest and told him who the baby's father was and that he had left Italy. They asked the priest what they should do with the child, since they did not want the responsibility of raising her. This child was a little girl who had been named Giovannina. The priest advised the parents to take the child to Donald Cuozzo and insist that he raise her, since he was the father.

Ship records indicated that Donald had come by himself to the Unites States. Since the girl's parents knew that Donald was no longer in Italy, they asked Raphaela to go with them to take the child to her father. We believe that is when Raphaela came to the United States. They took the child to Donald and asked him to take his child.

Raphaela spoke up and said, "Yes, he will take the child to remind him every day of his infidelity."

We believe that is the reason Jenny was badly treated—disliked by Raphaela and most of her siblings—and why she had no birth certificate. Maybe Jenny never knew who her real parents were. But now we know that she truly was a Cuozzo. That is why Jenny and Rosie looked so much alike—they were half-sisters. Johnny's search for the true identity of Jenny's parents has ended. Johnny is satisfied to know that she really was a Cuozzo. Donald was her true biological father.

Jenny undoubtedly never knew the truth but probably often wondered why she was not loved by the woman she thought of as her mother and most of her siblings. We know she was rejected because Raphaela's gravestone names all her children but Jenny.

And so ended Johnny's search to learn "Who is my mother?" And maybe the answer to "What was my purpose in life?" Perhaps it was to search and discover who his dear mother really was. And maybe someday he can tell her too.

The End

Julius and Jenny Mari's Children and Grandchildren

Baby Constintino

- died as an infant

Josephine

- born in 1922 and resided in Pennsylvania and Ohio
- married twice; second husband, Harry Yuckenburg
- five children, one from a previous marriage; also adopted a granddaughter
- suffered with polycystic kidney disease; died December 27, 1993
- daughter Judy Ann White died May 20, 1963

Constantino

- born October 26, 1924
- died in an accident at age 9, on August 31, 1933

Edward

- born September 30, 1926
- married Emma
- one son, Frank, who married Constance and had two sons; Frank is a family physician, both sons are attorneys

Rose Marie

- born May 24, 1928
- married Joseph Gautieri
- one daughter, Lucille, and five grandchildren
- died January 04, 1991

Julia

- born December 19, 1929
- married Joseph Broskin
- had three children and seven grandchildren
- died May 28, 1995

John

- born January 31, 1932
- married Priscilla (Patty Hodge)
- two children, Thomas and Susan; one grandchild (Nicole Lyn); and one great grandchild (Jacob)
- Susan died December 3, 1998

Constance

- born October 30, 1933
- married Mead Shank
- eleven children
- Connie (Mari) name change
- died March 8, 2008

Thomas

- born March 25, 1936
- married Eileen
- three children and one grandchild

Fredrick

- born October 13, 1939
- married Melonie (born May 23, 1942, died April 25, 1998)
- five children; one died at birth
- died April 24, 2001

Printed in the United States
By Bookmasters